W9-BIZ-755

Walking Home with Baba

The Heart of Spiritual Practice

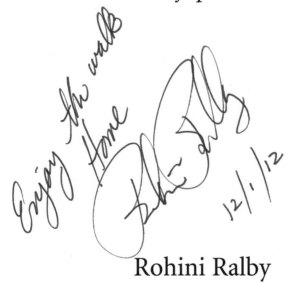

Rohini Ralby

**bancroft
press**

Copyright 2012 **Rohini Ralby**
All rights reserved.

No part of this book may be reproduced in any form or by electronic means,
including information storage and retrieval systems, without written permission
from the publisher, except by a reviewer, who may quote passages in a review.

Cover & Interior Design: Tracy Copes

Published by Bancroft Press
"Books that Enlighten"
800-637-7377
P.O. Box 65360, Baltimore, MD 21209
410-764-1967 (fax)
www.bancroftpress.com

ISBN 978-1-61088-057-2 (cloth)
ISBN 978-1-61088-058-9 (paperback)
ISBN 978-1-61088-059-6 (mobi)
ISBN 978-1-61088-060-2 (e-pub)
Printed in the United States of America

*To my Guru, Swami Muktananda,
who has given me everything*

Table of Contents

Preface

Spiritual practice will not make your problems go away. It will not make you and everything around you pleasant. It will not gain you power over others.

Spiritual practice *will* remove your ignorance. It will help you disentangle yourself from what isn't Real. It will reveal to you who you are, who you are not, and who you have always been. It will lead you to endless joy and love.

So what is spiritual practice? It is walking home. It is retracing our way back to the true Self. Until we do this, we will suffer, trapped within a false identity—our lower self, which is nothing more than a set of ideas.

To free ourselves from this misery, we must give up our false identity and remember who we really are. The true Self—our Real nature—is Absolute Truth, Absolute Consciousness, and Absolute Bliss. It has nothing to do with our personality, or any other temporary thing. It can't be perceived, because it is the pure Subject from which all the manifested universe comes. In different traditions, the Self goes by different names—God, Tao, Zen, Void, Real, Absolute, and so forth—but a mature spirituality recognizes that these names all signify the same thing.

There is only one place the Self dwells in us: the Heart. All great spiritual traditions locate God in the Heart. When Jesus said, "The kingdom of God is within you" (Luke 17:21), he meant it. In terms of spiritual practice, the Heart is not the physical organ or the seat of emotions, but the place within us where the Self resides. Our primary task, then, is to ground our awareness in the Heart and dissolve what prevents us from staying there. This means stilling the vibrations in consciousness that keep us from being our true Self. We start in the center of the chest, where we experience love. We then continue walking deeper inward to where we can know the true Self. Though this work is simple, it isn't easy. It takes many years of continual practice. At first, we may be able to get into the Heart, but we will be unable to remain there. Only after many years of diving in again and again will we be able to rest in the Heart. First we discipline our senses, then our minds, and finally our wills. The intensity with which we work through these stages is up to us.

Spiritual practice, no matter the tradition, unfolds through three levels. At the first level, we use our five senses and engage in outward activities. Chanting, looking at images and symbols, burning incense, and other physical rituals remind us of what is important. Care and moderation with food, steady posture, and exercises prepare our body for the rigors of meditation and spiritual awakening.

At the second level, we use the mind. Scriptural study, *mantra*, and remembrance encourage us to move our awareness inward and direct it toward the Heart.

At the third level, we use our will to rest in the Heart. When we surrender to the true Self completely, we are liberated from our shrunken sense of self, and we become who we truly are. Giving up our attachment to our individuality does not mean servitude to anyone; it means liberation from the tyranny of the lower self.

If you want to pursue spiritual practice, you will have to be willing to reflect, honestly and unflinchingly, on everything that makes up your false identity. Many people remain turned outward and never examine what they bring to the table. The practice of turning inward does not mean cutting yourself off from life. It means actively going deeper than our temporary vehicles—body, mind, personality, ideas, emotions, energy—and witnessing them from where you can recognize that they are separate from who you really are.

In the course of spiritual practice, your knowledge of what is true will mature. Your understanding will continually shift as you go deeper within. Time after time, your expectations will be shot down. What once seemed valid and important will be revealed as superficial and off the point. Your evolving discernment will show you how to proceed, allowing you to see more clearly the difference between what is Real and what is transitory. You must be willing to use every experience as an occasion for reflection and growth.

Surrendering to God is not easy. There will be times when you cling to your ideas and refuse to give up your limited sense of self. There will be times when you lose your way because the seeds of attachment within you have blossomed. Then you have to work even harder to regain your bearings. This cannot be accomplished alone. If you are to remain on the path, you will need the guidance of a capable teacher or spiritual director. Chapter Eleven will discuss how to assess prospective teachers, but the truth is that if you are sincerely committed to practicing, a suitable guide will appear.

I began walking home early in my life, not quite sure what path to follow. It was clear to me that I needed to go inward, but I wasn't sure how to do it. Until I could find a good teacher, I had to rely on my own effort. I learned discipline through school, sports, and especially dance. By the age of 21, I had focused on dance. My teachers at Washington University in St. Louis, especially Annelise Mertz, Leslie Laskey, and Nelson Wu, taught me how to see, hear, feel, and move from a place beyond thought or mere technique. When I moved to the San Francisco Bay Area for graduate school, I learned about Tai Chi Chuan and found another teacher in T. R. Chung. For the next year and a half, I worked with him intensively, often for several hours a day.

After graduate school, I returned to my hometown of Boston and opened a Tai Chi Chuan school in Cambridge. More than one hundred students came, and my school did well. Professors at Harvard, MIT, and Tufts invited me to demonstrate the principles of Tai Chi Chuan to them and their students, and a similar invitation came from the Taiwanese Consulate—quite an honor given that I'm not Asian. I also studied the Mandarin language and got a degree in acupuncture. After working in a clinic, I realized my distaste for needles and instead used my knowledge of acupuncture to aid my teaching of Tai Chi Chuan. At the same time, I learned Alexander Technique from Frank Pierce Jones, one of its leading practitioners. My teaching and my own practice often involved as many as 12 to 14 hours a day.

While practicing Tai Chi Chuan I experienced a powerful sensation of floating, wholeness, and freedom. I wanted the experience all the time, no matter what I was doing, but I found myself at the mercy of Tai Chi Chuan, and I could not get beyond it. When not practicing, I felt small and incomplete. Every year I spent a month in California studying with Chung to refine and deepen my Tai Chi Chuan proficiency. One August morning in 1975, I walked into his school to pay my respects and begin a month of study, and Chung said, "You're done here. Go to him."

"Him" was Swami Muktananda. How perfect! I was attached to my austere Chinese props, and disliked his colorful Hindu tradition. But he was the answer in every way. In order to break down the false self I had come to think of as "me," I had to find the Guru who defied all my expectations. What this did for me was separate the internal practice from external trappings and activities. I spent the next eight years with Muktananda as a member of his inner circle, going wherever he went. My time with Baba, as he was affectionately known, taught me exactly what I was looking for. I wanted to work only with him, and that desire was fulfilled. I was put in charge of security for the ashram in Ganeshpuri, India, I stood near him in the ashram courtyard, and I was his appointments secretary for most of his second world tour. Whatever needed doing, I did. All these roles taught me how to deconstruct my lower self and relate to the world as a human being rather than a personality.

Where I actually learned the practice, though, was by the back stairs of Baba's house in Ganeshpuri, where I stood alone with him as he sat on the steps. I learned how to be aware of my surroundings while constantly boring into the core of my being. Then I would rest there, as deep in as I could go at the time. I practiced everywhere what I learned by those back stairs. Silencing the thoughts and vibrations. Being still, so I could just be.

After the world tour, we returned to India, where he made me the librarian for the collection that included his own books. The library was always closed, so it was the perfect venue for me to deepen my practice. I would study, practice, and watch Baba in the courtyard from the library window.

Baba told me when it was auspicious for my then-husband and me to have a baby. When I was seven months pregnant with my first son, a *puja* (ritual) was held for the soul entering the womb. Two weeks later, on the full moon of October 2, 1982, Baba left his body. I had gone to see him earlier that day. He looked at me with unconditional love.

I will never forget each moment I had with him, whether he was instructing me by being kind, being still, yelling at me, or joking, which he did often. At every moment, he was showing me the Truth. He was modeling how to walk home.

The night Baba left his body, I had a tremendous urge to see him one last time. When I was allowed to, I went into his house and did a full *pranam* before his body, prostrating myself despite my advanced pregnancy. Baba had said I would have a boy and the birth would be easy. He wanted him born in India. So on December 9, 1982, my first son was born in Mumbai. It was an easy birth.

But I was angry that Baba had left me half-baked. I had experienced bliss in his presence, and I believed it was now gone because he was gone. After a while, however, I realized that it was I who had felt the bliss, so that bliss had to be inside me. Baba had taught me the practice; now I simply needed to do it, burn up the ignorance preventing me from knowing who I really was, and again experience the bliss I had felt in Baba's presence.

For many years, no matter what happened on the outside, whether giving birth to my second son, helping my two sons to manhood, or enduring and then leaving an unhealthy marriage, I just practiced, knowing that whatever God does, God does for good. Through all the years, Baba has been with me, guiding me on my walk.

This book is the expression of decades spent practicing and sharing the practice with others. Its purpose is to share how to free ourselves from misery and recognize who we really are. Though I will introduce a few tools I have developed over the years, such as the foursquare personality game and the process of stilling a seed, I will return again and again to the essential principles of practice.

To further clarify them, I have included a commentary on the most important aspects of Patanjali's *Yoga Sutras*. This ancient text involves terms that may be unfamiliar to you, but be patient; I will re-introduce and explain Sanskrit words to make them more accessible, and I have assembled a glossary that you will find at the end of this book. The *Yoga Sutras* are a useful roadmap. But a map is just a map; it is only the route home, not the journey.

I will also share stories from my own walk home that may be helpful both as lessons and as illustrations of life with a great Guru.

Though some of my lessons came from earlier teachers, it was Baba who led me home. He is still leading me, and he always will.

Chapter One
Preparing to Walk: A Map of the Territory

We all want to be happy. Where we look for happiness depends on who we think we are. The problem is that we decide who we are from a place of ignorance. We build prisons of personality, constantly seeking to define our identities by placing ourselves in boxes. We tell ourselves that we are successes or failures; that we are doctors, plumbers, teachers, homemakers; that we are parents or children; that we are tall or short; that we are ethnic in one way or another; that we are believers or nonbelievers. In trying to decide who we are, we cloak our true nature. Only by looking inward, beyond the instruments we enliven, and tracing our consciousness back to pure Subject, can we begin to strip away the veils of our wrong understanding. We must put personality, intellect, emotions, physical body, thoughts, and energy in their proper place: as outer vehicles of the true Self.

Happiness comes only when we know ourselves. Knowing who you truly are has nothing to do with any idea or feeling you have about yourself. If you think or feel you are one with the universe, then you are not. Knowing is being. The experience of who we truly are is bliss. When we touch on this experience, we usually feel relief, peace, and joy. This sense of wholeness is only a glimpse of Reality. When we live wholly in the Real, we live in Absolute Bliss, Consciousness, and Truth.

In order to get to this existence of Bliss and Consciousness, we have to give up something: our identification with the lower self. We have to give up our identity with our unique individuality and see it for what it is, an act performed by the Self. In the tradition of Kashmir Shaivism, we all share three impurities: the beliefs that I am imperfect, I am separate, and I am the doer of good and bad deeds. In truth, God is perfect, is one, and is the doer of all deeds. Turning to the Self is literally turning back to God.

We may turn back to God for many reasons. One reason could be that we are miserable and unhappy. Better yet, we are reflective and have questioned our goals and the source of our happiness. Reflection does not mean closing yourself off from the world; it means being cognizant of your inner workings.

As we grow more reflective, our understanding of God changes. For the spiritually young, God remains anthropomorphic, someone who can be depicted; God is Holy and Wholly Other—a localized object. For others, God has evolved into an idea, such as Love, Goodness, or Order. As a principle, God is still an object, still confined and separate. As we go deeper, God becomes an actual experience of Love. Though this experience is wonderful, we must come to know God as the pure "I am" of the Old Testament, beyond all qualities. Finally, we get to God's Reality as the pure Subject, the Self of All. At first, we may believe it, we may think it, we may understand it intellectually, but this is not enough. We have to *be* it. Each of us has to find the place where God is within us before we can experience God as All.

To accomplish this, we must disentangle from all our wrong identifications. From a dualistic standpoint, anything that is not permanent is not God—and that includes all the things we normally identify as aspects of ourselves, such as qualities, feelings, thoughts, and memories. They come and go, and they must be put into their proper places as tools we use, not who we are. Anything that you are able to perceive, including your inner experience, is not you.

The Yogic Map

Though in reality all is the Self, we have to live in a world of differences until we have achieved liberation. Patanjali's system of yoga is a useful guide here. It is only one of many maps in the world's religious and philosophical traditions, but I have found it especially helpful. In classical yoga, the Self is often called *Purusha*. Everything that appears not to be the Self—that is, the entire manifested universe, which exists for the sake of the Self—is known as *prakriti*. We must withdraw from our attachment to *prakriti* until we rest in our true nature, the *Purusha*.

Nearly every yogic tradition describes the manifested universe as composed of three constituent principles, or *gunas*: *tamas* (inertia, dullness, darkness), *raja*s (activity, agitation, passion), and *sattva* (calm, brightness, clarity). Nature is made of the nearly infinite combinations of these vibrations. A rock, for instance, has very little activity and a lot of inertia, while a storm is loaded with activity and has little inertia. To some degree, calm is present in everything, and when it predominates, we experience a serene stillness, as we might in the presence of a beautiful landscape. Our task in spiritual practice is to work our way to *sattva*, and then transcend all three *gunas*.

Like everything else in the manifested universe, our bodies are made up of the *gunas*. That principle is easy enough to apply to the gross physical body, but Indian philosophy establishes that we actually have four bodies: the gross physical body, the subtle body, the causal body, and the supracausal body. The first three bodies are a bit like nesting dolls, each subtler and deeper than the previous one; some Indic traditions refer to them as sheaths.

The gross physical body is what most of us call the body.

The subtle body is made up of the mind and energy centers, which include the *chakras*. It's worth noting that the subtle body is the size of a thumb and is located by going inward through the center of the chest, so anyone who tells you your *chakras* can be found in your gross physical body doesn't understand yoga.

The causal body is the vessel of *prana*, or vital energy. It also holds the stored impressions from our past actions. It is often said that this is where the breath begins.

The supracausal body both permeates and transcends the other three. It is where the Heart resides. In the Heart is the Self.

Each of the bodies is the venue of a particular state of consciousness. The waking state is linked mainly to the physical body, the dream state to the subtle body, and deep sleep to the causal body. The supracausal body is the home of the *turiya* or fourth state—the witness of the other three states. When we are awake, we use the physical body, the mind, and *prana*. In the dream state, we no longer use our physical body; we use our mind and *prana*. In deep sleep, we use only the *prana*. The fourth state is where who we really are resides. It is the witness that tells us about the three other states. It is witness consciousness.

Our psychic instrument, referred to above as the mind, has three components: the data collector (*manas*); the faculty of knowing, also called the intellect (*buddhi*); and the identifier, often called the ego (*ahamkara*). The psychic instrument functions in the field of consciousness, known in classical yoga as *chitta*. Remember that the mind is not who we truly are, but a vehicle of the Self. As such, it is properly called the lower mind or psychic instrument, because the higher mind is pure Consciousness. Through spiritual practice, we purify our vehicles so that they can be used as God wills. This means stilling the vibrations (*vrittis*) that unsettle consciousness. Until that work is complete, we are run by our wrong identifications and understandings. When vibrations reach the psychic instrument, they give rise to letters and words, forming thought-constructs. These thought-constructs are based on dichotomies that split the perceived into pairs of opposites: good or bad, male or female, cold and hot. As we practice, we will see the oscillating activity of the mind. Only when we have steadied the mind through discipline can we go beyond the relentless dichotomizing that prevents us from seeing our true nature.

Of the obstacles we face in our journey toward the Self, our attachment to our individuality is the most difficult. Personality is a combination of qualities, which really means that it is a set of thought constructs. Usually, we collect these ideas in our childhood. After years of being reinforced, they become the "facts" of our adulthood. The process of acquiring this combination of attributes is the birth of the lower self. We create this lower self, selecting and resonating with some qualities, "good" or "bad," and rejecting others, also either "good" or "bad." Buying into the lower self is making a leap of faith in the wrong direction. We suffer for it. While we make idols of our personalities, the true Self remains hidden.

The *Yoga Sutras* of Patanjali speak of the five afflictions, or *kleshas*, that have power in the lower mind where our lower self thrives. The afflictions are ignorance, ego, attraction, repulsion, and clinging to the life of the lower self. Each *klesha* feeds its successors. Ignorance is the root of the afflictions: it means taking what is not Real to be Real, what is temporary to be eternal, what is impure to be pure. Once we do this, we lose our subject in the object of our attention; we identify with something that is not our true nature. That wrong identification leads us to feel attracted to some things and repulsed by others. Finally, because we believe this illusion to be our Real selves, we cling to it for dear life. We fear the death of this small self. We maintain a miserable existence without recognizing that we made it for ourselves.

The Heart

Spiritual practice, the only way out of this misery, is really the discipline of self-surrender. It is a way of living, not a fix that makes us feel better for a moment until we return to our habitual way of operating. As I mentioned in the Preface, the main work of spiritual practice is grounding your awareness in the Heart. This isn't an idea—it is the actual practice of bringing your consciousness and attention into the center of your chest. From there, you bore inward as far as you can, and rest. At any given moment, the deepest place where you reside is effectively who you are. Everything you can now perceive needs to be stilled. Once you complete the process of stilling what is in front of you, then your mistaken sense of self becomes perceptible as an object, and is no longer you. You are then able to dig to a deeper resting place, where you experience, "This is who I am." You continue the process of stilling what is perceptible until you reach the Perceiver, which is pure Subject with no object. This is the Self, and where it resides is the Heart. You need to go there, and to remain there as constantly as you can.

You can practice at all times and in all places. When she first began, one of my students felt good when she was in class but could not practice successfully elsewhere. She was convinced that one could not practice at the mall. So we got into the car and drove to the mall. In the food court, which was packed and noisy, we sat at a table in the middle of the whole sensory experience. We began to practice. Though nobody would have noticed us doing anything in particular—we just sat there without even closing our eyes—we shifted our attention inward and grounded it in the Heart. My student saw that at our table all was quiet, and that the chaos and noise had receded. She could in fact have success practicing in any environment. Spiritual practice does not mean hiding in caves, but engaging in life appropriately—from a place of Truth rather than ignorance.

Gaining Non-attachment and Discernment

To engage in life appropriately, you need a sense of humor. Believing that your individual story is precious and serious will leave you unwilling to let go of it. When you achieve non-attachment, laughter quickly follows. You will begin to play your part in the universe rather than be your part. Baba had a great sense of humor, and loved to play with us and tease us. He encouraged us to give up our attachment to how important we thought we were, so that we could be free to enjoy the play of the universe. By working to be absorbed in the Self, we became less self-absorbed.

With that in mind, we can see that spiritual practice is anything but selfish. You do not withdraw from activity in the world, but from attachment to the world. Only when you have cultivated two qualities essential to spiritual practice, non-attachment (*vairagya*) and discernment (*viveka*), can you actually serve the world effectively. Non-attachment and discernment support each other: the more you free yourself from attachment, the better you can distinguish between what is and is not Real. When you practice service from the lower self, your motives are impure and your actions tainted by self-interest. When you act from a place of non-attachment and discernment, the love and compassion within you can express themselves purely. The point is to strive for such perfect non-attachment that your discernment never errs, and you never do injury to others or yourself.

The bird that flies to God, it has often been said, has two wings: right effort and divine grace. Right effort is crucial. It isn't the apparent effort of the physical body or other vehicles, but the constant surrender to the Self. If you practice this, divine grace will draw you to God.

Until you attain complete non-attachment, you will be subject to the laws of karma. Karma is simply the law of cause and effect, which operates throughout the manifested universe. As individuals, we collect karma through attachments. Every action arising from attachment generates an effect on us, further binding us to the manifested universe through bad, mixed, or good karma. As we travel through our lives, we have to reap what we have sown.

Awakening

Divine grace first appears in the form of an awakening. In my spiritual tradition, this experience—the descent of grace—is called *shaktipat*. *Shaktipat* awakens the *kundalini*, the spiritual energy coiled in the subtle body, which remains dormant until activated, sometimes spontaneously but usually by a spiritual teacher. A teacher transmits energy (*shakti*) into a student through touch, word, look, or intention, and that transmission stirs up the *kundalini*. The student's awakening can range from mild to intense. It can generate a feeling of peace and joy, an experience of fire and heat, physical shaking, changes in breathing, intense bliss, visions and sounds, heightened senses, spontaneous laughing or weeping, or extreme agitation. Every spiritual tradition acknowledges this critical moment in the journey toward God, but few work with it in practice.

Shaktipat is only the beginning of internal work; if you want to walk home, you must undergo a conversion. Converting literally means turning around—in this case, turning inward, in a complete reorientation of your life. If you have already been working to prepare yourself for conversion, then it may well arrive with *shaktipat*. If you haven't, then *shaktipat* will only be an experience of powerful energy and supernormal sensations. Without the right effort of inner surrender, an awakening dries up, leaving only a set of concepts, not a living practice.

Your practice will change as you grow more into the Truth. You are walking a path that requires you to revise your understanding as you move along. You grow to see what is Real and what is temporary in each of the different levels. Where previously you got caught up and identified with whatever disturbances arose, you have now learned to be with your experience, let whatever comes up come up, and function appropriately. You see that what once appeared Real is obviously temporary. You learn that what appears Real will soon be revealed as temporary. Only when you let go of everything, surrender to God and rest in the Heart will you be the Self you truly were all along. You will be *sat-chit-ananda*: Absolute Truth, Absolute Consciousness, and Absolute Bliss.

You will have arrived home.

Chapter Two
Stories of Early Teachers

I had been up all night finishing a paper, but I felt compelled to go to dance class. Before my parents separated when I was 14, I studied dance every day; after, there had been no further dancing until college. During my second semester of modern dance at Washington University in St. Louis, I was working hard on technique. There was always a sense that we wanted to go beyond technique, but every time I went across the floor, my movements were stiff and self-conscious. Annelise Mertz, my teacher, would always say, "No."

When it was time to go across the floor, Annelise showed the combination, and we began to take turns going across to a driving drum rhythm. When my turn came, I was so exhausted I couldn't even think. I danced across the room without thought. I was completely aware—not self-conscious, and not unconscious, but purely conscious. My body was weightless and free, yet under perfect control. When I got to the far side of the room, Annelise looked at me and said, "It's great, isn't it?" She knew. I knew. At that moment, I understood what it meant to let go of technique. It wasn't about having no technique; it was about mastering technique and then letting it just be. Complete control comes from complete surrender. Annelise had been pushing me to learn this. Once the lesson was accomplished, she didn't yell anymore. She didn't say, "No." For her, it was never about mere technique. It was always about dance.

Annelise also worked with us on composition and improvisation. She constantly berated us, telling us that we were wrong, that our compositions were contrived, that our improvisations were forced. She embarrassed us in front of each other. Her real purpose was to strip away our attachment to and identification with our ideas of "good" dance. One day she turned to me and said, "Get up there and show us." I had thrown together a study on one leg and didn't want to perform it.

"Do I have to?" I asked.

"Yes."

I finally just gave up and did it. By that time, I knew how to dance, not just execute techniques. When I finished the composition, Annelise looked at me and simply said, "Yes."

What I learned from her was the process of not thinking in action. Being in the zone. Sharing the joy of dance. Of course, my problem was that I thought I could have this experience only through dance. I did not know how to transfer it to the rest of my life.

———— • ● • ————

Some of my important teachers were not, conventionally speaking, teachers at all. They were people with whom I crossed paths, in encounters that served as learning experiences. In college, I was once walking back from the Wash U campus to my apartment at dusk. It grew darker as I walked. An old, dark sedan pulled up beside the curb. The window was rolled down, and it seemed that the man driving wanted directions.

When I walked up to the passenger door, he leaned toward me and said, "Get in the car."

"No," I said.

"Get in the car."

As I stood there, I found myself looking down the barrel of a handgun, and for the first time experienced the stopping of time. In a deep calm, I felt myself expand into that timelessness. Everything was heightened and clear, and I seemed to be witnessing the entire scene from above. I looked at the gun. I looked at the hate in the man's eyes. I said to myself, *Raped and shot, or shot? Shot.*

Returning my attention to the man, I said, "No. Shoot me, then." I turned my back to him and walked slowly away, never looking back.

———— • • • ————

In Leslie Laskey's design seminar at Wash U, about ten of us would drive around St. Louis looking at things—art, buildings, parks—and then discuss everything from aesthetics to construction techniques. For Professor Laskey, the crucial thing was feeling the objects, not thinking them. Everything we examined had its own music, and our task was to sense that music and respond to it. One day, we wandered all over town looking at wrought-iron fencing. On balconies, along streets, in front of houses, every length of fencing was unique. Each stretch of ironwork had its own weight, its own rhythm, its own aesthetic—its own feeling. Professor Laskey forced us to look at the most mundane things in a way that freed us from all our preconceptions and allowed us to experience every object we examined as a unique statement.

———— • • • ————

In his course in Asian art and architecture, Nelson Wu didn't want us just to memorize information, he wanted us to experience the art. In one class, he began with aerial photos of the temple complex at Borobudur, then, through a series of photos, walked us into the place. In another, he shared with us the greatness of a single stroke of Chinese calligraphy. I still recall him standing by the slide, saying, "Such a moment. It's so alive, so present." We saw how each stroke conveyed the inner state of the calligrapher at the moment he put brush to paper. Though I didn't get to know him personally, Professor Wu showed me what it meant to be a true scholar. He didn't just deal in information and ideas, he shared with us how he experienced great works of art.

———— • • • ————

After graduating from Wash U, I moved to Oakland, California to pursue an M.A. in dance at Mills College. During my first year there, it dawned on me that I had spent my education dancing other people's choreography but had never discovered my own dance. My body was now an instrument that communicated in many languages, but I had no idea what my own native dance was. During a six-month span, I would lie on a studio floor for hours at a time, waiting to feel my own dance emerge. When it finally did, it was a slow, liquid series of movements, each flowing into the next. When I performed it, someone told me that it reminded them of Tai Chi Chuan. I had never heard of Tai Chi Chuan, but a little research led me to Berkeley, to the small storefront studio of T. R. Chung. I signed up there and began practicing rigorously.

I decided one day to perform the dance I had choreographed. No one was there apart from Chung and me. Afterward, Chung asked where I had learned that form. He thought it was a martial arts form from a different lineage of Tai Chi Chuan than his. My direction was clear. I worked hard to learn the Guang Ping form he had inherited from his teacher, the great master Kuo Lien Ying. While gradually teaching me the form, Chung also had me practice "standing meditation," in which I had to hold an upright position, with my arms extended as if around a big ball, for long periods of time. I had no idea why he required it, but I practiced it. I had learned over the years that I really didn't know anything, and that obeying my teachers didn't mean giving up my own discernment.

One day in his studio, he told me to begin standing and hold the position. Resigned, I settled into my stance. As an hour passed, waves of energy began rising and circulating in me. Looking inside, I could see the energy as white light, and was able to move it around within my body. *Oh*, I thought, *that's why he made me practice this.*

Standing meditation had helped me become aware of my *chi*, the subtle energy cultivated and directed in Tai Chi Chuan.

After a year of working several hours a day on my Tai Chi Chuan, I had learned the form to Chung's satisfaction. He told me to go teach. After earning my Master's degree, I was offered positions teaching dance at universities, but instead I returned to Boston and opened a Tai Chi Chuan school in Cambridge. Once a year, I returned to Berkeley to work with Chung for a few weeks.

———— • • • ————

While teaching Tai Chi Chuan in Boston, I constantly tried to expand my knowledge. I took a degree in acupuncture and worked in a clinic, studied Mandarin, and practiced Chinese calligraphy. I also decided to study another form of martial art, Hsin-yi. In the spectrum of martial arts, Hsin-yi is a bit more external than Tai Chi Chuan. My Hsin-yi teacher, Mr. Li, had a loft in Chinatown. Three or four times a week, I would go there, and he would instruct me in the form.

Mr. Li was in his eighties and lived by himself, and though he was considered a master and had tremendous *chi*, it was clear that he was lonely and unhappy. He smiled a lot, but after a while, I couldn't help but feel something negative in him.

One evening, the day before I was going to start studying Aikido, another form of martial art, I went to watch a Chinese martial arts movie. Seated several rows in front of me, by himself, was Mr. Li. The movie was typical of the genre: betrayal, revenge, and lots of violence and death. Looking at him and at the movie, I knew that I didn't want to end up like Mr. Li. I quit studying Hsin-yi, never started Aikido, and began looking for something more. Though Tai Chi Chuan was wonderful, it couldn't take me where I now wanted to go. I didn't know where to turn.

———— • • • ————

Frank Pierce Jones and I had a bargain. I taught him and his wife Tai Chi Chuan, and he taught me Alexander Technique, a method of re-establishing the body's natural posture and movement. In the course of working together, we also sent each other students.

Frank taught through his hands. They were magic. Their gentlest touch would free me from my physical boundaries. Through Alexander Technique, he helped me reestablish my body's natural way of moving. I had to start from scratch, with sitting and walking. Only after several months of work was I allowed to talk while doing these things. Eventually, I got to the point where I could walk and sit while reciting passages from *The Adventures of Alice in Wonderland* and *Through the Looking Glass* and feel completely weightless.

We met twice a week for two years, until one day he tripped during Tai Chi and lost his balance. Though the misstep looked like nothing, it was the first sign of the brain tumor that eventually took his life. After his surgery, I visited him in the hospital. It was a wrenching experience. Frank had been so vital even in his late seventies, and now he was feeble. Facing mortality, this classics professor lay in his hospital bed reciting poems about death by Donne, Blake, and others. He died shortly after. When I went to his funeral, I was so distraught that I couldn't face his family. I've always regretted that.

Part of Frank's legacy to me is a story of his I have never forgotten. He had gone to see a performance by the great mime Marcel Marceau. While performing, Marceau was perfect: totally conscious, completely present, utterly real. But after the show, when he came out to answer questions, he wasn't present at all, Frank said. His movements and responses were absent-minded, disjointed, uncoordinated. That story reminded me of myself. I had been able to achieve a level of mastery in my practice of Tai Chi Chuan, but I couldn't carry over that perfection into the rest of my life. I wanted to experience that connectedness all the time—not just while practicing the form, but while washing the dishes or walking down the street.

———— • ● • ————

In Boston, my Tai Chi Chuan school flourished, but I grew increasingly dissatisfied. More and more, I experienced internal chaos while practicing Tai Chi. I felt a relentless, all-consuming interior burning. Though I could see my *chi* circulating through my body like blood through my veins, and could even channel it at will, my mind felt out of control when I wasn't practicing the form.

One night, I dreamed that I had no soul. Intellectually, I knew it wasn't true, but it felt so real that the most honest thing to do was admit it. I announced to my students throughout the day the truth that I had no soul. By the end of the day, it was as if that reality had sloughed off, and I could laugh about it. In facing and accepting what I experienced as true, I dissolved it.

———— • • • ————

I first heard of Baba in December of 1974. Someone told me that a man named Swami Muktananda was coming to Boston, and a few of my students were going to see him. I was indifferent. I had my path, I thought, and in any case preferred the more austere aesthetics of China and Japan to what I saw as the florid style of India. Instead of seeing Muktananda, I would go on a vacation to Jamaica. The day before leaving, I went to meet a friend at the place where Baba was to speak. I waited for a long time in the meeting hall, sitting on the floor near Baba's chair and some of his paraphernalia. My friend never showed up, and I left before Baba arrived. In Jamaica, I dreamed of a little Indian man in an orange robe, and couldn't get him out of my mind. Only later, when I saw Baba's picture, did I realize that he was the man I had seen in those dreams.

Throughout the following spring, I couldn't seem to get away from this Muktananda. Many of my students and friends had become his devotees, and they gave me records and books by and about Baba. When one of my friends was in the hospital dying of leukemia, people gathered in his room and chanted Indian *mantras* that Baba had taught them.

Later that summer, I went on my usual trip to study more with Chung in Berkeley. When I walked into his studio, he scarcely looked up.

"You're finished here. Go to him," he said.

I walked out of his studio in shock, only to see on a lamppost a flyer advertising Baba's Oakland ashram. I called and registered for a month-long retreat.

I first saw Baba in person as he got out of his car at the ashram. I was hoping for something dramatic, but it didn't happen then. In the meditation hall, I was put off by the bowing, adoring crowd of seekers and devotees, but I took a seat on the floor. As Baba turned his head in my direction, I saw a brilliant blue light shoot out of his eye and enter mine. A jolt of energy rushed through my body, like a shock of chi. I was surprised, but it wasn't different from the energy I had already experienced within myself.

———— • ● • ————

From early childhood onward, I often experienced energy. In many cases, it took the form of lights, colors, and out-of-body events. Sometimes at night, I would project a tiny blue light from within myself onto the wall of my bedroom. It was somehow comforting to see, and it would occupy my time until I drifted off to sleep. Once, during a family trip to Ohio, I became conscious that I was dreaming a nightmare and forced myself to wake up in the middle of the night. When I awoke, I wasn't in the hotel in Ohio, but in my bedroom at home. The lights were out, the bed was made, and the house was empty. I knew that my body was somewhere else, but I was in my house. The only thing to do was go back to sleep so I could wake up back in my physical body, so I let go, drifted off, and awoke in the hotel room.

As an adult, I found that some people were drawn to what they saw as my spiritual power. Students in my Tai Chi Chuan classes felt my *chi* strongly; I was able to lay my hands on people and heal them. I experienced heat shooting up and down my spine. To me, it was all part of Tai Chi Chuan, and I simply told my students to keep practicing. Once, a fellow Tai Chi Chuan teacher who had studied for years in Hong Kong remarked, "Your kundalini was awakened." I didn't understand what he was talking about. I did know that my practice of Tai Chi Chuan had generated internal power, but that power wasn't making me happy. I wasn't looking for power. I wanted to understand the bottom line of existence, and I wasn't getting there.

When Chung sent me to Baba, I happened to have enough money to take the month-long retreat in Arcata, California. For years, I had been bothered by a pressure and lump in the middle of my forehead, between my eyebrows, accompanied by a vivid white light. I was racked with internal heat much of the time. During one daily session at the retreat, I mustered the courage to walk up to Baba and ask him about my forehead. He took my head in both hands and pulled me close. Then he lowered his glasses, leaned close, and gazed into my eyes—or, rather, into me. I could tell that he saw all of me, right into my core, to the Self that I couldn't see. Looking into his eyes, I saw the entire universe open up, a vast space filled with brilliant light and deep darkness. Baba made a fist and ground his knuckles into my forehead, and then let me go.

By the time I had returned to my seat, I could feel enormous energy welling up from somewhere within me. Seated, my body began shaking, jumping, moving, and breathing rapidly without my control. I saw brilliant lights going in all directions inside me, and felt electric currents surge through me. This was a new kind of energy—not only more intense but of a different quality than any I had experienced before.

Before, my mind would wrap itself around the experience of the energy and make an idea of it. Now, I experienced myself as separate from what was happening. Even as I watched my mind and body react, I was calm in the certainty that those vehicles were not who I was. In the complete peace of that moment, everything made total sense, and there were no more questions. I knew that I had finally experienced my true Self. Baba had given me the greatest gift I had ever received. I knew I had found the teacher I had been searching for.

Chapter Three
The Three Levels of Spiritual Practice

When we speak of spiritual practice, most of us think that everyone is doing the same work, no matter where they are in the process. This is like mistaking an apprentice for a master; both may look the same, but they are working at completely different levels. We tend to assume that other people are practicing at our level, so we never ask what their actual practice is. Using the same words, such as "yoga" or "meditation," does not mean practicing the same thing or at the same level.

When we are told that every tradition has three levels, we are surprised. We usually think that there is only one level, and that experts just work best at that level. But no first-grader who knows her addition and subtraction facts, scoring perfectly on her flash cards, should be encouraged to believe she is a mathematician. There are, in fact, three levels of spiritual practice, and we must work our way inward to the third. The *Siva Sutras* of Kashmir Shaivism, the writings of St. Simeon and other Orthodox Christian hesychasts, and the letters and lessons of some Sufi teachers, for example, all testify to this crucial, but often overlooked, reality.

First-Level Practice

First-level practice uses the five senses, focusing them on objects that remind us of God so that we can reorient toward Reality. In first-level practice, we look at certain objects, taste certain foods, wear certain clothes, smell certain smells, and so on. We may also prohibit certain foods, sights, clothes, smells, and the like. Elements of worship such as icons, rosaries, malas, incense, shawls, robes, hats, chanting, movement, breathing exercises, music, hymns, candles, architecture, stained glass, altars, ablutions, and rituals of any kind are all components of first-level practice. We participate in these rituals as individuals, addressing God as Other. First-level practice, then, aims to form a relationship between the individual and God through the senses and through action.

A rich first-level experience will involve objects on which each of the senses can focus. A solemn mass—which includes music, chanting, kneeling, oral prayer, breath awareness, incense, highly visual sacraments and vestments, and an expressly sacred space— can be beautifully uplifting. It can make you feel exalted. But if you believe this exaltation is as good as it gets, you cut yourself off from a chance to see that there is something more. If you go to a *hatha yoga* class where instructors talk about mind-body-spirit, *chakras*, breath control, and so forth, and you leave the class feeling calm and restored believing this is as good as it gets, then you are mistaking sensory experience and exercises for the deeper practice necessary to attain union with the Self. There is nothing wrong with going to a *hatha yoga* class, but it is delusional to think that it offers the highest level of practice. No matter how advanced the class, it's still first-level work at best. The emotional thrill or exalted feeling we may experience during these rituals arises from the sensory experience of the ritual, and it will fade when the props are removed.

Because the first-level deals with the senses and the physical body, it deals also with forms and temperaments. Any external system has its rules, which are not necessarily universal. Different cultures and subcultures may prescribe different external practices. The robes of one culture will not be appropriate for another culture. The Jesuits, for instance, have been known to modify their robes depending on the culture in which they are working. At the first level, a tradition can absorb external forms from other traditions. For instance, the Christmas tree came from pagan culture and was integrated into Christianity. Today, some people might feel that they won't be Christian if they don't have a Christmas tree.

The props we use in first-level practice need not come from a religious tradition at all. Any physical activity that disciplines the body and senses will work. Taking a walk, working out, playing sports, dancing, gardening, practicing hobbies, and even cleaning can serve the function of first-level practice, in which one begins to discipline and quiet the body and mind. Many of these activities are incorporated into monastic life for just that reason.

But the forms and temperaments of the first level can divide us from others. When we focus primarily on outward forms and prescriptions, we miss the point entirely, often to the detriment of others and ourselves. Fighting over who has the right outfit, place of worship, or rule book means forgetting God entirely. There have been great beings who practiced and did not wear brown robes. They wore maroon or orange ones. They wore black robes with white hats. They wore orange *lunghis*. They wore Western street clothes. They had no hair, long hair, wild hair, braided hair. They chanted in Sanskrit, Hebrew, Latin, Greek, Russian, Arabic, English, and any number of other languages. They sat cross-legged, sat in pews, stood, knelt, or prostrated themselves. They gazed at icons, statues, Torah arks, gardens, or crosses. The common denominator here is that all these practices are representational. They are invitations. They are the means by which we enter deeper practice. They are not the universal inner practice that all these great beings shared. If we remain at the first level, no matter how proficient we become, we will remain far from our goal.

What first-level practice should lead to is a feeling that there must be more. There is more, but not on this level. Going to a different tradition's first level will not get you anywhere. It's like thinking you will get a better view by going into the ground floor of another building. This is why many traditions remain restrictive in their first-level practices, rejecting any forms and prescriptions but their own. When people wander among different first-level practices, picking and choosing, they only get confused. They get entangled in the first level.

Once again, there is nothing wrong with the first level, as long as we don't think it is the goal, or that it alone will take us to the goal. Spiritual practice is not a track meet where each level exists like a lane alongside the others and each can take you to the final goal. If done properly, each level will lead you into the next. First-level work succeeds by leading us to the second level of practice, which in turn leads us to the third.

Only by practicing the third level can we reach union with the Self. If we believe that first-level practice will lead us to God, we will end up angry and frustrated—because in truth, the first level is worldly. In first-level practice we remain dependent on the outside world to provide a sense of God's presence for us. If we feel we are only with God at our place of worship and not at the mall, then we have a limited awareness of God. As a result, we may only practice when and where we believe God is present, and forget that God is always with us. At the first level, we are separate from God, and separate from each other. We can start here, but we must not remain here.

Second-Level Practice

If, having worked hard at the first level, you feel there is something more, then you may become aware of a second level of spiritual practice. At the second level, we use a different, subtler vehicle—the mind. Second-level practice is about knowledge and energy. Scripture study, reflection, constant remembrance of God, internal use of *mantra*, and working to shift our awareness from the head into the Heart are all aspects of second-level practice. We use the mind and work to master it, mainly through words.

Words limit us, but what limits us can also help liberate us. Unless you understand the power that gives words their ability to shape your world, you will have no control over your own mind, and hence no control over your life. If, on the other hand, you comprehend that power, you can understand the workings of your life. The right words, with the right energy behind them, can take us toward the Self. This is why *mantra*—a group of letters forming a sacred sound that protects us and helps us return to the Self—is often a key part of second-level practice. *Mantra* repetition does not mean rote recitation; it requires one-pointed concentration. With steady practice, it leads to a deep understanding and aware-ness of how Reality is manifest in sound.

Whether it is a Sanskrit phrase, a Hebrew prayer, a Buddhist formula, or the Jesus Prayer, internal repetition of a *mantra*, when done correctly, will call the name of God. A call from the first level, as no more than part of a ritual, will not reach where God meets us; a call from deep within will. If someone calls your name from close enough that you can hear, you will respond. If we work our way inward enough, closer to the Self, and call God's name over and over, God will respond, and we will be able to hear. God is still Other in second-level practice, but we have approached closer. There is a saying that a thousand recitations from the tongue are worth one from the mind, and a thousand from the mind are worth one from the Heart.

The goal of second-level practice is to move the mind out of the head and into the Heart. The effort to make this shift, using knowledge and energy, is the essence of second-level work. We are taught to regard the brain as the foundation of the mind. In truth, the brain is the outer mechanism that expresses the mind on the gross physical level. Consciousness actually resides in the Heart. Put another way, second-level practice is working to overcome the habitual delusion that the mind should be in the head. We must constantly bring our attention out of the head and down into the Heart, where the Self resides.

To master and transcend the mind, you have to have it in front of you as an object that you can perceive and let go of. You can only accomplish this by withdrawing inward toward the Heart, deeper than the mind. To identify with the mind is to be controlled by it. When you are identified with the mind, your thought-forms rule your life, distorting your perceptions and causing you misery. And this includes emotions.

Emotions are actually thought-forms with goo on them, and regarding them as better or worse than more "intellectual" thought-forms assigns them a value they don't deserve. Only when you have gone beyond this false distinction can true feeling emerge. Most of what passes for feeling in our lives is, in fact, sentiment, which is a particular kind of emotion. We are lost in our minds and, according to our dissociative programs, turn outward and away from the source of our emotions, suppressing real feeling and substituting imitation "feelings" that are acceptable to the lower self. In second-level practice, we turn inward and move toward the Heart, deeper than our emotions. From there, we can see emotions properly as objects, remain non-attached, express them appropriately, and begin stilling them at the source.

There are detrimental and beneficial sides to second-level practice. As always, we have to walk the path with non-attachment and discernment. At the first level, the harm is done when we believe that outward forms and rituals are sufficient. Here at the second level, the danger lies in believing that the "right" ideas, insights, or feelings are enough. Even worse, we can become prideful about our knowledge and decide that our theories, ideas, and self-understanding place us above those around us. In truth, at the second level, we only *know about* the goal. We think the goal, and the words with which we think only obscure the goal, which is beyond our intellectual understanding. The thought-form, "I understand the highest Reality" is not where we want to be. The highest Reality cannot be limited to a thought form. We must go beyond all thought-forms to uncover our true Being. Second-level practice can take us to the brink; then we must jump out of our thoughts to reach the third level.

The second level continues to move us toward Reality. It helps us center ourselves, resolve the dichotomizing activity of the mind, and focus our attention into one-pointedness. It will not take us all the way to liberation, but it will take us further than the first level. As St. Simeon said about this level of practice, a moonlit night is better than a moonless one.

Third-Level Practice

At the third level, our practice is so completely internal that there may be no outward sign that we are practicing at all. While first-level practice involves primarily the senses and second-level practice the mind, the third and deepest level of practice uses the will. Second-level practice has allowed us to arrive in the Heart. Now we exercise our will to remain there.

Many people misunderstand this level. Because they can't get past believing the Heart is the seat of emotion, they think that if they feel deeply or practice earnestly, they are at the third level. You must remember that the Heart is where the true Self resides. It has nothing to do with our individuality, or anything temporary. It isn't personal. In order to get there, we have to drop our attachment to all our vehicles. Once there, we can maintain stillness.

Getting to the Heart is difficult, but resting there is effortless. When you consider how much effort goes into maintaining the lower self, you can see that remaining in the Heart is actually being at rest. There is no effort because we are no longer the doer. The Self is the doer, and we rest in the Self. This doesn't mean we don't engage in life. Instead, we are fully alive.

When we are in the Heart, we practice *sahajsamadhi*, or walking bliss, which entails being within the Heart and looking out at the world at the same time. From this place, the play of the universe becomes a joyous delight.

Having walked this far, we can see clearly how we got here. At the first level, we used external supports and performed rituals. At the second, we used internal supports and moved inward using the mind. At the third, we use no support and simply will ourselves to remain in the Heart. Though we may still engage in first-level and second-level practices, we will do so from a much deeper place, and that depth will transform our actions. Only when we have reached this level do we have a chance of attaining liberation. Remaining in the Heart and stilling all vibrations, we will be who we really were all along: the All.

Chapter Four

Stories of Baba, 1976-1977

In the spring of 1976, we were staying at the DeVille, a converted hotel in Fallsburg, New York. I had already heard from a number of ashramites about what, in their minds, Baba liked and disliked—what to do and what not to do.

When I was working security, walking around in the sun all day, I got a deep tan. It didn't bother me, but a woman who had been at the ashram for a long time said, "Baba doesn't like women with suntans." On another occasion, the same woman said that Baba didn't like women with short hair.

I missed my practice of Tai Chi Chuan. One day I went out into the field and did the Tai Chi form. The president of the organization attached to the ashram saw me and approached as I finished.

"That was beautiful," he said. "It was so beautiful."

Tears welled up in my eyes. "I was told that Baba wouldn't like me doing that."

"Absolutely not!" he said. "That's not true. Baba would love you doing that. Baba doesn't have that attitude. Baba would never want you not to do that."

People often made judgments about trivial things. Baba didn't care about any of it. At no time did he like me more or less because my hair was long or short, or because I was tanned or fair, or because I was or wasn't practicing Tai Chi Chuan. It was all off the point. What mattered was that I was healthy, non-attached, and practicing my *sadhana*.

Many of the people who carried around such petty judgments had been in the ashram for years. Baba called them "old shoes." I considered them my equals, my guru brothers and sisters. The idea that they were somehow speaking for Baba was ridiculous. Baba was the only one who could speak for Baba.

———— • ● • ————

At the DeVille, I attended all the intensives. During these programs, I sat at the back of the hall, by the door. I sometimes went so deep into meditation that, though I was totally conscious of the activity around me, I was resting in stillness and bliss. Once, I remained sitting there all day. Lunch and the afternoon program came and went, and people vacuumed around me during cleanup. I knew exactly what was happening but remained in bliss, just sitting there. This sort of meditation happened to most people at the ashram, so it was no big deal.

———— • ● • ————

Even as a child, I thought of myself as a warrior. When I owned and ran my Tai Chi Chuan school, I very much lived out that ideal, holding events such as weekly sparring sessions among different schools. It was such an integral part of the way I manifested that I wouldn't let go of it easily.

After receiving *shaktipat*, it wasn't until the winter of 1975 that I returned to the Oakland ashram. There had been a rash of robberies and a few muggings, and when I volunteered to do *seva* (service), I was assigned guard duty. I would stand on the roof of the ashram and keep an eye on things, or drive around the neighborhood for hours to make sure things were safe.

The following spring, when I moved into the ashram full-time, I volunteered to do security, and I would recite *mantra* internally while walking the perimeter of the property. I would also stand by the gate where Baba entered and left the evening program, so he passed right by me. Even a simple greeting from Baba had a heightened quality, so I appreciated the chance to be near him even that much. By being there every night, I developed a more personal relationship with him.

That fall, we went to Ganeshpuri, and it was there that I formally became head of security. Baba told me not to be afraid to hit anyone, and handed me a stick. Thirty men worked under me, including some Ghurkas who called me "boss." We worked in shifts to keep the ashram secure. On one occasion, 2,000 Adivasis came to the ashram, and I organized the crew to herd the visitors down a path to see Baba and receive clothing and water buckets from him. I also had to keep mangy, sometimes rabid, dogs out of the ashram, mainly by throwing rocks at them. Baba called me Ganesh, the gatekeeper. Even when I had malaria and was quarantined, my crew would come to my window to report and to take orders. I was the disciplinarian. Part of my job was to go with Baba on his afternoon walks and keep people at a respectful distance.

When Baba finally said to me, "You're done with this. Now stand in the courtyard and talk nicely to people," the whole system of ashram security faded. The job had existed so that I and others could work out karmic issues.

———— • • • ————

The first time I had the opportunity to enter Baba's house in Ganeshpuri, I had no idea why he wanted me there. I found myself in a small sitting room with several other people. No one explained why I had been summoned. Everyone sat in a circle on the floor; I was next to Baba. Baba's valet translated as Baba, skipping over me and starting with the person to my left, told each person in the circle what they had done wrong in terms of *ashram dharma*. In the process, he occasionally yelled at people, but they usually felt chastened, not scorched.

Everyone accepted their rebuke silently, except for Amma, a former Sanskrit professor who had been with Baba for more than twenty years. When Baba scolded her for reading newspapers—he always said that reading newspapers and magazines was trading in gossip—she laughed. Baba ignored her response. A couple of times, Baba asked me whether the person he was chastising had said or done something in particular. As head of ashram security, I was often asked how much I knew about who had done what, when, and where.

When Baba had completed the circuit, he dismissed us. I wondered why Baba had wanted me there. In retrospect, I saw that this event was my introduction to an inner working in the ashram I had not been privy to. Before that incident, I had never seen Baba get angry or yell, and I had never understood how much he cared about everyone's *sadhana*.

———— • ● • ————

It was the hot season of my first year at Ganeshpuri. I had come to know the different kinds of ashramites, and among them were non-Indians who had no visa issues and had stayed at the ashram for a long time. One of those people, a wealthy Englishwoman living alone in a cottage, had come undone. She was no longer bathing, cleaning her space, or taking care of anything, including herself. She had reached a point where she was both depressed and aggressive, and she clearly needed to go home.

Baba told another woman and me to pack up the English-woman's things, see that she bathed, take her in a car to Bombay, and get her to the office of a devotee who worked in the Indian government and could get her on a plane for England. The task wasn't easy; she was much taller than I and stronger than my relatively fragile partner. We sat her between us in the car as the driver took the two-hour trip into Bombay. At one point during the car ride, the Englishwoman bit my arm. After I pulled away, she quieted down for a while, until suddenly she reached across and opened the door in an attempt to leap out of the moving car.

When we got to the office of Baba's devotee, we were told to wait. There were no plane tickets, and we sat outside his office for hours waiting for a meeting that never happened. Finally, someone told us to go spend the night at the Holiday Inn Juhu Beach, which was owned by another devotee and was close to the airport. Neither I nor my companion had expected this; we had been told to take the Englishwoman into Bombay and return, so we had no change of clothes or toiletries. It took some calming and convincing for the Englishwoman to agree to stay at the hotel.

The next morning, nothing still had been done. We had no plan, and no one had contacted us. The Englishwoman lost her patience. Saying, "That's it, I've had it," she walked out of the hotel and down the driveway toward the center of Bombay. At the bottom of the hotel entrance ramp, I blocked her way and took hold of her arms. It was a typically crowded Bombay street, and instantly we were surrounded by scores of Indians intrigued by the spectacle of two Western women facing off. As I held her arms, I tried to convince her to stay, but she was determined to leave. After a few minutes, I realized how ridiculous the situation was and hit my limit.

"Fine. Go. Leave," I said, and let go. The Englishwoman ran off, jumped into a cab, and disappeared into Bombay. I stood there feeling as if I had done something wrong by letting her get away, and everyone at the hotel shared that perception.

My companion and I spent the rest of the day at the hotel, waiting for something to happen. Nothing did. No one contacted us. Eventually, another woman from the ashram showed up and told us to return to Ganeshpuri. After another night at the hotel without a change of clothes, we drove back.

When we arrived at the ashram, I immediately went to the office of the ashram manager. With tears in my eyes, I told him what had happened. He laughed good-naturedly at my earnestness. I was new at the ashram, and didn't understand the *lilas,* or plays, that went on there. Gradually, it dawned on me that what had happened was precisely what everyone had wanted. They had wanted to let her go, because her family was so politically powerful that no one could touch her. The only way to deal with her was to take her into Bombay and let her go. Had I known the plan, I might not have played my part so well. As it happened, she left on her own terms, under her own power. Eventually, she found her way to some Catholic nuns, who arranged for her to collect the rest of her belongings at the ashram and then fly home.

I never encountered her again, but received word she was fine once she got home.

———— • • • ————

Baba would sometimes ask me to check up on people at particular places and times. One day in Ganeshpuri, Baba called me to his room and told me to go to a particular man's room at a precise time, knock on the door, and then tell Baba what I saw there. By that time I already knew things were seldom simple, and this man was something of a VIP—one of the ashramites who had a "hands off" status.

When I knocked on the door, he answered, and behind him was a much younger woman. It was clear that something illicit was going on, and he was furious that I had found him out and disrupted whatever was happening. The man had no idea that Baba had asked me to come.

It was always like that: everyone assumed that Baba was too "spiritual" to concern himself with such things. It never occurred to them that he might have known all that was going on. People assumed I was a busybody, nosing around where I shouldn't. They never realized that Baba asked me to check on things in order to teach me the ways of the world and teach them whatever lessons they were to learn.

———— • ● • ————

One night, there was an event in the upper garden at the ashram in Ganeshpuri. Gatherings were rarely held there, and afterward everyone would descend from the upper garden and cross a bridge to the rest of the ashram. The afternoon before the event, Baba told me to wait near the upper garden side of the bridge after the program and tell him what I saw there.

It was pitch dark by the bridge, and hundreds of people were passing by. I had no idea what I was looking for, so I just stayed alert. Suddenly, out from behind a large bush appeared the shadow of a man. He leaned out, whispered something to a passing woman, and returned to his hiding place. The woman continued walking as if nothing had happened. No one else appeared to have seen him, and people continued flowing past.

I reported what I had seen to Baba, and within two days the woman was sent home. The man, as it turned out, was a worker, not an ashramite.

I found myself sitting with questions. Why did Baba want me to see that incident? Did I really see it? Would I have seen it had Baba not told me to look? It happened so quickly, in such a dark place, that I had trouble believing it was real. But, as the outcome revealed, something had happened, and Baba had known it was going to happen, and he had wanted me to witness it.

———— • • • ————

When I was still in charge of security, one of my jobs was to walk around at the beginning of every chant or during *seva* and make sure people were doing what they were supposed to be doing. It was fascinating: the ashramites had professions outside the ashram—doctors, lawyers, academics, executives—but, confronted with the relentless schedule of the ashram, they would do all sorts of crazy things. They constantly attempted to get out of the steady work of scriptural chant and *seva*. Those activities grind down the ego, and sometimes people just cracked. My job was to keep discipline, keep herding people back to the ashram activities.

The ashram dorms had flat wooden beds with thin mattresses, and underneath were baskets in which ashramites kept their clothes. Time and again I would find people hiding in those baskets, trying to avoid some ashram activity. Or they would be hiding behind trees in the upper garden. I always found it ironic that people were avoiding precisely the activities that would do them so much good.

Everything got pared down at the ashram. Things were so austere that people argued over the simplest issues. Before chanting the Guru Gita at 5:30 every morning, some tried to set their cushions by the wall and then go get tea, expecting to be able to sit against the wall during the chant—only to find that their cushions had been moved by other ashramites. We had to make a rule that if you weren't on your pillow, it could be moved, so people would skip tea to ensure that they could get their choice of seat. Such things as the size and kind of broom someone was handed, and whether or not Baba gave you flowers took on a ridiculously outsized significance, and Baba used them to teach us lessons. Everything was designed to help our *sadhana*.

If we couldn't handle the little things, we couldn't handle the big ones. If I couldn't manage to organize a bunch of pillows, how could I expect to organize a board meeting in a corporate situation? It was about learning how to master one simple thing, and then gradually adding other responsibilities. If we could stay in the Heart while doing the smallest things, we could build from there. In that regard, many people used the ashram as a retreat, to reorient themselves before returning to their customary lives.

———— • • • ————

In Ganeshpuri, a lawyer who had come to the ashram from New York was assigned as *seva* the job of shoveling and carting buffalo dung in the upper garden. One day, as he told me later, he was complaining to himself while working. "I'm a lawyer. I should be doing significant work. This is insulting!"

At that moment, Baba walked by with some visitors. Pointing approvingly at the lawyer, he said, "That man is a lawyer. See, he's doing good work."

The lawyer suddenly understood that, in a community that had to grow its own food, carting buffalo dung for fertilizer was actually important work. That experience in humility freed him.

———— • • • ————

While making my rounds one day as head of ashram security in Ganeshpuri, I came across a group of Adivasi workmen shouting and throwing rocks at something in one of the vegetable patches in the upper garden. A huge rat was eating the vegetables and moving about erratically. It was obviously rabid. The tribesmen were trying to kill it without getting closer than a few feet away.

Not pausing to think, I picked up a rock. Without my throwing it or exerting any conscious effort on it, the rock rolled out of my hand and struck the rat, killing it instantly. The action took only a moment, and felt effortless, completely natural and ordinary. The Adivasis, though, were almost as excited by what they took to be a minor miracle as they had been by the rabid rat itself. Afterward, I was amazed as well. I hadn't been aware of aiming or throwing the rock. It had all just happened.

———— • ● • ————

While I was head of security, a young man who had been assigned to guard duty was always late for his shift. He was cocky and smug, and refused to take the job seriously. Despite having been reprimanded many times for his irresponsibility, one day he didn't show up for work at all. In his absence, I relieved the guard whose shift was ending. His post was opposite the main entrance to the ashram.

After a while, I saw the ashram elephant coming down the road, returning from its daily exercise. Sitting proudly on its back was the young man who was supposed to be on duty. He grinned and waved as he rode on by. Several minutes later, he finally sauntered up to me at his post, confident that his negligence would go unchallenged. I looked him in the eye and said, "You're late." Then, without anger, I punched him in the stomach, knocking him to the ground.

Stunned at being hit by a woman, he threatened to report me to Baba. I told him, "Be my guest."

Just as I had been free from anger when I punched him, I was free of anxiety about the consequences. I was responding to the situation without rigidity. Time would tell if I had acted appropriately.

He was never late again, and afterward he dropped at least some of his attitude.

Chapter Five
*Seeds: Recognizing the Vibrations
That Make You Miserable*

Gaining an intellectual understanding of spiritual practice is one thing; actually doing the work is another. To begin the return home to the true Self, we need to dismantle the lower self. And to deconstruct something properly, we must know how it works and how it first took shape.

Many believe that, in order to understand the lower self, we have to sort through our childhood experiences. Such reflections have their place, but spiritual practice is about how we manifest through our vehicles in the moment. Anything we need to learn from our childhood is right in front of us in the present, distorting our perceptions, and the present is where we will do our work.

Everything in the manifested universe begins as a vibration. That includes all our thoughts, feelings, and sensory experiences. Vibrations of all kinds, both pleasurable and painful, imprint our vehicles. These vibrations become the mental habits and attachments that make up the lower self. In our ignorance, we believe that our personality is who we are, so we cling to it. Our lives then begin to look like soap operas, in which characters never grow and, instead, live out the same experiences again and again. Consciously or unconsciously, we love our vibrations. Sometimes we love to hate them. Often, spiritual growth only begins when we get bored of them.

To describe how vibrations work, scriptures often use the metaphor of the seed. A seed is the manifestation in the mind of a vibration that has become an unconscious habit. In favorable environments, seeds grow. When conditions are ideal for them, they blossom, pervading all our vehicles and setting our consciousness vibrating ferociously. Eventually, every seed must be starved and then burned up. But that comes late in the process. Most of the time, seeds remain buried and therefore unnoticed—until the right circumstances appear. Because we are attached to and identified with the vibrations that constitute our personality, we believe that the flowering of a seed is an expression of our true nature.

In our ignorance, we fail to separate the vibration from the mind and the mind from the Self. In the Yoga Sutras, Patanjali establishes that, in the state of ignorance, the modifications of the mind appear to be the Self (*Yoga Sutras* 1.4). Of course, things only seem that way to our intellect, which is, after all, veiled by attachments. Once we see a seed for what it is, we can do as Patanjali instructs in sutra 2.10: trace it back to its source as a vibration in the Heart and then still it.

We live in a culture that encourages us to believe emotion is somehow more real than thought. Whoever conveys the most intense emotion is considered the most genuine. As a result, people often lose all discernment, worshiping emotionality and even emotional hysteria. Non-attachment and discernment are seen as cold and unfeeling. Working to burn up seeds will require you to disentangle from your emotions. This does not mean refusing to feel; it means not being identified with your feelings.

To recognize your seeds, you have to stop looking outside yourself for the causes of your unrest. Ordinarily, we see ourselves as reacting to apparent causes in our environment; in truth, those seeming causes are merely occasions for us to manifest a seed already within us, waiting to be expressed. We need a process for gaining control over a seed. Over the years, I have developed such a technique.

As a first step, you must be reflective enough to notice that something within you is distorting and disturbing your perceptions. This can be extraordinarily difficult, because seeds can alter your perceptions completely, yet remain undetectable to you—though often obvious to those around you. When you are thinking or behaving in a way that requires you to rationalize and justify your choices to yourself, then you are dealing with a seed. If you find yourself in the midst of an internal experience that feels familiar but out of your control, you can be sure that you are looking at a seed. This feeling arises because to be under the spell of a blossoming seed is essentially to be possessed by a vibration. If you listen attentively, you can feel it. Once you detect a seed, though, you have already begun to disentangle yourself from it.

The process of stilling these vibrations goes from the outside in, and unfolds in a series of steps. Where you start in the sequence depends on how far off track you have allowed your seed to lead you. Regardless of where you start, it isn't easy. Often, it involves the pain of facing a delusion that has run your life.

Here is the entire process:

1. Recognize that you are confronting a seed.

2. At this point, it is better not to talk about it. Talking about a seed indiscriminately, before you have disentangled from it, keeps you in it.

3. Allow yourself to be enveloped in the seed *consciously*. Do not try to deny or suppress it.

4. Put a name to the seed.

5. Recognize that the seed pervades everything you see and do.

6. Reflect on other times you have experienced the seed, whether or not every instance makes rational sense.

7. Ask yourself, "Do I always have this experience?" Once you recognize that you do not always have it, you can see it as separate from who you are.

8. Objectify the seed: disentangle from it and ground your awareness in the Heart. The vibration will begin to quiet.

9. Witness as the vibration loses strength and you no longer feel compelled to act on it.

10. Stay in the Heart and be vigilant so you can catch the vibration earlier the next time it arises.

One of my own seeds might serve as a good example. A few years ago, two years after undergoing surgery, chemotherapy, and radiation for breast cancer, I went for my annual pelvic ultrasound to check for possible side effects from the post-treatment medication I was taking. Two days after the ultrasound, my doctor called and told me that the lining of my uterus had thickened from 2mm to 8mm, and that I needed to come to his office and discuss what we were going to do. I couldn't get an appointment for another full week. Instantly, I found myself in despair. I felt a sense of powerlessness in my gut and a deep vibration of hurt in my chest, and then the thought-forms started coming. I didn't see any possibility of not having cancer or only having pre-cancer, or even a chance of localized uterine cancer. My mind went all the way to uterine cancer that had spread throughout my body.

I had felt all this before and worked on it, so I knew I was experiencing a seed I had already put a name to: "Donna Despair." That acknowledgement was the first step in attenuating the seed, which had blossomed as soon as the doctor called. I could have decided that I was "fine" after acknowledging the seed, but that would have solved nothing. I would simply have been numbing myself to my own experience instead of resolving it. From my own practice, I had already learned that stilling the vibration of a seed is much more difficult than simply acknowledging it and trying to turn away. The next step was to allow myself to be with my despair consciously and not run away from the experience. That meant a willingness to inhabit the vibration: "Hi, I'm Donna Despair. Who are you?" Paradoxically, only by consciously inhabiting the experience was I able to separate out of it and objectify it.

In the course of that week, I allowed myself to be with the experience of despair and recognize how it could color everything I saw and did. My external circumstances didn't make any difference; whether teaching, visiting my son at graduate school, or just going for a walk, I could witness my mind seeing everything through the lens of despair. On further reflection, I was able to connect my current experience of despair with other times in my life when the same seed had manifested. The other episodes hadn't called for despair, but I had felt it nonetheless. The seed had sometimes blossomed in circumstances that didn't make intellectual sense. A seed doesn't blossom only on obvious occasions. At the same time, it was clear that I didn't always have this vibration, so I knew it was impermanent and therefore not truly Real.

There is no way to still the vibration of a seed through reason. I could understand intellectually that the seed was something separate from me, but I knew from experience that the only way to deal with a blossoming seed is to trace it to its root—the Heart. If we still the vibration there, then thought-forms will never emerge from it. So I sat with the vibration at its source, detached from it, and watched it lose its strength and then disappear. I had starved it of attention by withdrawing from my head and grounding my awareness in the Heart. By the time I arrived at my doctor's office, the despair was stilled and I was ready to deal appropriately with the issue.

No matter where in the process you start, you must allow your-self to consciously experience being immersed in the vibration of the seed. You must neither deny it nor judge it. It is just a vibration, not who you are.

Here's another example that might help clarify how this works. A student I'll call Gail constantly victimizes herself with the seed of misery. She has made a mental habit of believing that being happy means being selfish, so the only way she can see herself as a good person is to reject happiness and be miserable. Of course, this seed is mostly unconscious. Once Gail recognizes that her misery is a choice, she can objectify it as something separate from herself and put a name to it. When Gail is caught in the seed, the delusional thoughts it generates seem utterly real and true to her, so it will help to give the seed a silly name—in this instance, "Molly Misery." The silliness of the name reinforces the unreality of the seed and allows Gail to separate herself further from it.

With a little separation, we can see that, when the seed is blossoming, it pervades all of our experience. Gail will begin to recognize that when she is caught in "Molly Misery," everything is an occasion for misery, no matter where she turns. This realization hurts. It is nothing less than recognizing a way in which she has deluded and diminished herself for much of her life, to say nothing of the ways in which her seed has led her to hurt and disappoint others. But to judge herself and linger in regret and self-recrimination would be to remain in the seed, using her practice as just another occasion for misery. The point is to still the vibration.

After seeing the pervasiveness of the seed, we can then inventory all the occasions when it has manifested and recognize that our seed, not external conditions, is the common denominator. The unavoidable question then is, "Is this seed always blossoming?" The answer to that question is, of course, no. And if it isn't always blossoming, it can't be who we are. With that realization, Gail can separate even further from her seed of misery and get a sense of its overall shape. Molly Misery's features become clearer, and hence more distinct from Gail herself.

At this point, Gail is ready to disentangle herself fully from the seed, redirect her attention into the Heart, and ground her awareness there. Instead of being identified with the seed, she redirects her energy and starves the seed. She can then witness as the vibration goes still and the seed disappears.

What remains after a seed has been stilled is vigilance. You must rest in the Heart and stay conscious of what emerges there. After all, resting in the Heart anchors you at the point of contact with God, where all things emerge within you—including seeds. You must remain in the Heart to still vibrations before they blossom. In the Heart, you can choose not to be caught up in a seed. If, on the other hand, you live in your head, by the time you recognize a seed—if you even recognize it—it will already have hijacked your experience, and you may have done injury to yourself and others.

As you pursue this practice, you will be tested repeatedly with occasions for seeds to come forth; old habits die hard. In some instances you will get lost in seeds yet again. But if you persevere in the practice, you will gradually gain a sharper awareness of each seed as a delusion and attenuate it. Like a boater going downriver, you will learn to hear the rapids ahead and choose to row ashore rather than be swept into treacherous waters. Spiritual practice is no more and no less than the moment-to-moment, day-to-day grounding of your awareness in the Heart.

Chapter Six
Stories of Baba, 1977-1978

One day during the hot season, an Indian man was caught stealing money—a few hundred rupees, which was a fair amount—from another Indian man in an ashram dorm. The police were contacted and the man was caught. Baba called me into the courtyard and told me to go to the lower garden where a bridge extended over the paddies to the upper garden and watch what happened there. This was during the hottest part of the day, just after lunch, when everyone retreated to their rooms to hide from the heat. No one was around.

By the bridge, I found a policeman standing before the thief, a hardwood baton in his hand. The two men formed a silent tableau in the shade of a stucco building. Beyond the line of shadow was brilliant sunlight. The policeman raised his baton and the thief bent over to receive the blows. With the baton, the policeman beat the thief mercilessly about the back and shoulders. The thief crouched down under the blows, his arms wrapped over his head.

Though I stood only a few feet away, neither man acknowledged my presence and no one uttered a sound. It was a silent performance. Both men knew the story and their roles in it. The officer's job was to mete out immediate punishment; the thief's job was to accept it.

I was tired of being head of ashram security. I had always seen myself as a warrior, but by the time of this incident, I had grown disenchanted with that form of expression. By having me witness the beating, Baba was helping me let go of the anger folded into my sense of myself as a warrior. The policeman did his *dharma*. The thief did his *dharma*. The beating was an instant, quick administration of justice. Afterward, the policeman took the thief to be expelled from the ashram, and that was the end of it.

———— • • • ————

During the monsoon of 1977, one of my tasks as head of security was to make sure mangy dogs didn't get into the ashram. I blocked the ashram gates with wire mesh, but the dogs were still getting in. Then I discovered that they were coming in through the drainage pipes in the upper garden. I had to wade into the dense vegetation there in order to block those passages. Afterward, I began to feel ill. I thought it was the flu. A homeopath in the ashram agreed, but every two days, in the early afternoon, I got worse.

Baba sent the head of Kaliyan Hospital and a couple of other doctors to my room to examine me. The doctors concluded that I had an amoebic abscess. They wanted to take me to Kaliyan Hospital, a crowded, fly-infested facility nearby. Not knowing that one of them was the chief of Kaliyan, I said, "I'd rather die than go to Kaliyan Hospital." They reported their diagnosis to Baba. Though I had been taking chloroquine, he advised them to treat me for malaria.

The next day, I was sicker than ever. I felt as though an elephant were standing on my chest. In the hundred-degree heat, I couldn't stay warm. When I wasn't freezing, I was burning up. My temperature hit 106°F. I lay on my bed wrapped in six blankets, and still my teeth chattered.

Suddenly, I was out of my body, looking down from near the

ceiling. I was no longer an individual. Everything was still, and everything was perfect. I could see my body on the bed, but it was as if my seeing was everywhere, and I was everything. Then a decision was made—simply made, not by me—that I would return to my body. Back in my body, I opened my eyes and looked through them.

At that point, Baba declared that I had drug-resistant malaria and that I was to be quarantined in the ashram and treated with pure quinine. He established my regimen. I was fed only chapati with no oil, and boiled vegetables with no salt or spices. The only thing I was allowed to drink was the water from the boiled vegetables. The quinine nauseated me terribly and made my ears ring constantly. Since it was the monsoon season, everything was mildewed and I couldn't bear the smell of my mattress, so I had someone take it away and I slept instead on the wooden board of my bed. I often lay in the fetal position on the stone floor in a corner of the room. At one point, I was given anti-nausea pills, but they agitated me so intensely that Nursie, Baba's nurse, stayed with me until they wore off. I so appreciated that.

The ordeal went on for about two months. Once I felt a bit better, I organized security shifts by talking to my crew through the screened window of my room. When I finally left my room, my chest was caved in, and I couldn't stand up straight. I weighed less than 100 pounds. I walked into the dining hall where Baba was about to give a talk, and he was happy to see me. I was even happier to see him, and relieved.

I knew that the malaria was a karmic event. The ordeal burned up a tremendous amount of anger in me. Once I recovered, I knew that running security was no longer right for me, and I waited for the opportunity to move on.

It turned out that I had suffered from two kinds of malaria at once: *falciparum*, which is the most deadly, and a milder form that remained in my system and would resurface annually. From that time on, Baba unfailingly kept me supplied daily with a papaya and bitter melon, which contains natural quinine. Even on the world tour, he made sure that papayas and bitter melon were provided for me.

The following year, when the malaria returned, I was weak. Baba gave me a vile-tasting but effective ayurvedic medicine, and insisted that I come and stand near him at the back stair. He wanted to make sure that I didn't fall into being sickly. Baba saved my life, and then he worked for years to keep me healthy.

———— • • • ————

Baba often gave me gifts that went against my aesthetic. When I was in charge of security, Baba gave me a sandalwood stick with a silver tip. To me, it looked like an antique table leg. He said to carry it around, so I held it while on security, even though I would have preferred a simple bamboo stick. Another time, he gave me a silver snake ring. The gift that made me most uncomfortable was a large silver cuff bracelet with an image of Ganesha. "You're Ganesha," he said, "so use Ganesha." He sometimes called me "General," and wanted me to dress accordingly. When we went to New Delhi in February 1978, I was looking forward to wearing saris, but Baba told me to wear suits. I ended up wearing a long khaki skirt with a short-sleeve shirt and vest. Baba was having me dress according to my inner sense of myself, so I could detach from it.

During Guru Purnima that year, thousands of people came from all over India to pay their respects to Baba, despite the fact that it was the middle of the monsoon and everything was wet. My job was to stand close to Baba and control traffic, making sure anyone who came to see Baba followed the right route and kept moving. I directed the women, who were on a separate side from the men. Guru Purnima is a very important, festive day, and an auspicious one for seeing a guru, so everyone dresses in their nicest clothes; the women wear their best silk saris and their finest jewelry. I was planning to do the same, especially because I was going to be positioned prominently in the courtyard helping direct the proceedings.

About five days before Guru Purnima, Baba handed me a sari to wear for the occasion. It was made of white cotton damask, lovely and simple, but it was not a special-occasion garment. And white was usually worn only by widows and *brahmacharyas* (renunciates). I went back to my room disappointed. Once again, he had forced me to detach from my idea of how I wanted to appear. Without saying a word, I wore the sari. Many of the ashramites looked at me oddly because no one knew it had come from Baba. After that lesson, I let go of my attachment to clothing as an expression of my vocation, role, or inner state. Baba never prescribed any particular clothing for me again.

———— • • • ————

In Ganeshpuri, I used to stand near Baba by the back stair of his house every day after lunch. Baba would sit on the steps, and either he would meet with people or he and I would just be quiet. It was when Baba and I were alone together there that he taught me the practice. While he lived it, I practiced it. Though outwardly I was looking at him, inwardly I was boring into the Heart and then resting there, still and quiet. There would be no thought, just stillness. That was how I connected with Baba. I would stand and he would sit for however long he wanted to be there each day. An onlooker wouldn't have seen anything happening, but Baba was teaching me.

During the monsoon of 1978, when I suffered my second bout of malaria, I stayed in my room for a few days, and Baba began asking where I was. He knew I was sick, but he wanted me at the back stair for my sake.

Sometimes Baba wouldn't want anyone to come to the main courtyard and he would just sit as I stood nearby. There, too, I practiced looking out and going into the Heart simultaneously, being still. It was so clear what the work was.

Back when I received *shaktipat*, I had known that Baba was the teacher who could give me what I wanted, which was to be with God all the time, day or night, no matter what I was doing. And Baba showed me all the time, through mundane activity, how to do it. It wasn't sitting in full lotus position or anything like that. It was an internal process undertaken regardless of external activity.

Chapter Seven
The Foursquare Personality Game:
A Way Beyond Limited Identity

Every mystical tradition, regardless of its particular form of expression, explains existence in terms of Absolute Reality and relative reality. At the end of every path, we realize that everything is One, but that Oneness is nothing but a nice idea until we have reached the state in which we *are* that Unity. Until then, we operate only in relative reality, where we do the work of dismantling our lower selves.

The lower self is nothing more than our identification with our physical bodies, our thought-constructs, and any other qualities or objects. We look outward to see ourselves when we should be asking who is looking out. Though the true Self is, in reality, looking out at our intellect and the rest of the manifested universe, we believe that our intellect, our faculty of knowing, is our core self. You may recall that the lower mind, or psychic instrument, is made up of the data collector (*manas*), the intellect (*buddhi*), and the ego (*ahamkara*). The data collector brings in information, the intellect makes decisions about that information, and the ego identifies with those decisions. The intellect operates by creating dichotomies, and the lower self attaches itself to these dichotomies, deciding what is "good" and what is "bad." Those attachments shape our personalities, which then trap us.

The *Siva Sutras* explain the process of bondage through the *matrika shakti*, the power inherent in letters and words. From birth, we are encouraged to differentiate, particularize, and judge through words. We choose words to assess and express our inner and outer experience and then we consciously, or unconsciously, attach our sense of self to the words we have chosen and the qualities they symbolize to us. Our attachment to those words may take the form of attraction or repulsion.

Yet the *Siva Sutras* also establish that the *matrika shakti* is a means to liberation. By grasping its power, we can deconstruct the prison we have made for ourselves. That deconstruction begins with recognizing the dichotomies that make up our shrunken sense of self. We may have hung our identities on such qualities as competent/incompetent, attractive/unattractive, smart/stupid, or sensitive/insensitive. Whatever our dichotomies, we must see them for what they are. It is no coincidence that *matrika* is connected to the Latin word *matrix;* the words we identify with become the matrix of our limited, impure sense of self. Our lower self is then nothing more than a collection of words that may or may not coincide with the manifested world. We constrict ourselves into seeing and behaving according to that fixed set of ideas. This is the true prison-house of language.

We choose the words with which we identify; the *matrika shakti* puts energy into the words we have chosen. We then become objects defined by those attributes. Within each attribute lies the potential form of its opposite—and also of the positive and negative terms that shadow each attribute in our lower minds. Someone attached to the dichotomy of "lazy" and "hardworking" also will have issues with words like "easygoing" (the positive of "lazy") and "consumed" (the negative of "hardworking"). Once we are attached to a quality, we will work to create an environment within and around us that perpetuates that quality. If we refuse to accept the opposite of the quality with which we identify, then we will "hire" someone to embody that quality so that we can experience it as wholly separate from us.

For instance, if we are attached to being hardworking and refuse to acknowledge our own ability to be lazy, easygoing, or consumed, we will look to surround ourselves with people we can think of as possessing those rejected qualities. Our rigid, shrunken sense of ourselves and of how life works is then ruthlessly enforced. Ironically, we want to be a contradiction in terms—a changeless ego—instead of the all-encompassing pure Subject that is our true nature. In order to dismantle this prison of objectification, we have to comprehend and accept the whole system, both positive and negative. Until we accomplish this, we will judge all our experience through the lenses of our false identifications.

Once we have recognized a dichotomy or related set of dichotomies, we must accept all the terms connected to each dichotomy completely and unreservedly. Only when we have owned them fully can we transcend them. "Owning" means accepting that we, in fact, have each quality in a dichotomy. We may consciously or unconsciously choose to use it. (Not that using a quality unconsciously lets us off the hook; we remain responsible for all our words and actions.) Once we have fully owned all the qualities, we are then free to discern when, where, and how to manifest them appropriately. We also begin to recognize that, rather than objects that change, such as our feelings, our thoughts, our qualities, our experiences, or even our energies, we are in truth pure, unchanging Subject: the Self of All.

None of this will work unless we learn how to truly listen to ourselves. We have to start where we are, not where we would prefer to be. What we usually consider "listening to ourselves" is merely paying attention to the endless chatter of our lower minds. Instead, we must go inward toward the Heart, the core of our being, to hear our true responses. We must withdraw our attention from our outer senses and our mental machinery and literally turn inward to our center. At first, we don't hear our true answers so much as feel them or perceive them inwardly. With experience we eventually hear them clearly, as if with our ears, or even see them as if spelled out before our eyes. This practice has to be developed; otherwise we hear our true answers only as whispers drowned out by the din of mental chatter. And the lower self will waste no time distorting all our true answers to fit its agenda, so we must hear them instantly and without mental spin.

Until we have achieved complete non-attachment and therefore pure subjectivity, our answers will change from moment to moment. That means we must hear each answer *in the moment*. To answer in a general, abstract way is to respond from the wrong place entirely. Not recognizing that our answers will shift all the time shows once more how we delude ourselves into thinking that our lower self is constant and unchanging, when in truth it is anything but. Only when we have transcended any and all attachment to a particular set of qualities will our answers stop changing. We must transcend not only our attachments to "bad" qualities, but our attachments to *all* qualities, because all these false identifications bind us.

When we have learned how to hear our true answers, we can begin to practice a method of freeing ourselves that I have developed as a spiritual director: the foursquare personality game. Imagine a woman named Ann, who is anxious about having been called "lazy." Her anxiety reveals her attachment to that word. To free herself, she will have to identify and own the entire cluster of qualities she has arranged around "lazy" in her own mind. She will have to listen inwardly for the words she has consciously or unconsciously chosen to include in that cluster of identifications.

First, we set up the foursquare grid. As indicated below, the quality at issue goes in the upper left quadrant. Its opposite will go directly across from it.

Negative Characteristics	Positive Opposing Characteristics
Positive Forms of Negative Characteristics	Negative Forms of Positive Characteristics

Ann is struggling with the hurt she feels from having been called lazy. Because "lazy" is the dominant false identification for Ann at the moment, it goes in the upper left.

Lazy	

To Ann, the positive opposite of "lazy" is "hardworking." It goes in the upper right quadrant.

Lazy	Hardworking

Here is where things get subtler. The lower mind never stops at one simple dichotomy—hence the foursquare approach. Ann's cluster of qualities will include the positive form of "lazy" and the negative form of "hardworking." First, Ann must listen for her own positive form of "lazy." In her case, what comes up is "easygoing." This word goes in the lower left quadrant.

Lazy	Hardworking
Easygoing	

Now, Ann must discover her own negative form of the quality "hardworking." She uncovers "consumed," which fills the lower right quadrant.

Lazy	Hardworking
Easygoing	Consumed

At this point, Ann has something to work with. Her task is to own, and to be okay with owning, all four qualities in the grid. She must repeatedly ask herself, "Am I lazy? Yes or no? Am I okay with that answer? Yes or no?" The same questions follow for each of the four qualities. Again, knowing how to listen inwardly is crucial: she must answer the questions in the moment, without any mental spin. To think the questions through at all—a process that almost always leads to the wrong answer—would override her true, unalloyed response in the moment. The goal is to be able to answer "Yes" to every question, at least ten times in a row, on a regular basis. When Ann reaches that point she will have at least temporarily freed herself from her bondage to the word "lazy" and the other words she has linked to it. She will be free to choose to be lazy, hardworking, easygoing, or consumed, as appropriate.

For Ann, what eventually surfaces is how her definitions of seemingly simple words are, in fact, emotionally charged and deeply flawed. Like all of us, she has assumed that her definitions of these words are in harmony with everyone else's, when in truth she has manipulated definitions in order to create and sustain her lower self. Now that she has owned all four qualities, she can see how she has mislabeled people, their actions, and herself. For instance, she never before wanted to be "hardworking," because, for her, it was emotionally bound up with the dictionary definition of "consumed." Because she had been unwilling to own "lazy," she had neglected her work but thought of herself as "easygoing." That tendency to confuse and conflate definitions dominates our lives when we function from the mind instead of the Heart. In the case of a negative quality, we either refuse to own it or worry that we have it. Both responses are pure delusion, because we contain all qualities. And we should be attached to none of them.

It's often easy to identify the negative qualities we cling to. Just as treacherous spiritually, though, are the positive qualities with which we construct our lower selves. Consider Mike, who has come to identify himself with a set of pseudo-spiritual virtues. Once again, we construct our grid, only this time with the positive qualities in the upper left.

Positive Characteristics	Negative Opposing Characteristics
Negative Forms of Positive Characteristics	Positive Forms of Negative Characteristics

Mike considers himself sensitive, intuitive, humble, trusting, peaceful, and free. Some people might find nothing wrong with that set of qualities, but, again, the point is not to be attached to any qualities at all. Our true nature is the Perceiver, not the perceived. So Mike must listen within himself for the words he has clustered around the qualities with which he identifies.

Sensitive	Cold
Intuitive	Concrete
Humble	Arrogant
Trusting	Skeptical
Peaceful	Aggressive
Free	Trapped
Emotionally volatile	Clear-headed
Dreamer	Realistic
Falsely modest	Confident
Gullible	Reflective
Inert	Assertive
Irresponsible	Responsible

Mike's identification with the qualities in the upper left quadrant, as well as his idea of himself as a "good" person, will require him to deny or deflect from himself the other qualities in the grid. He will attract people who embody for him the qualities he refuses to own, and he will unconsciously express those qualities in his own behavior. Ironically, Mike's very identification with being "free" boxes him in.

The first scenario might play out in any of his relationships. At work, among friends, or even in his marriage, Mike might find himself constantly engaging with people who in his mind are cold, concrete, arrogant, skeptical, aggressive, and trapped. In the same way, he might attract people he can think of as emotionally volatile, falsely modest, gullible, inert dreamers. Though he might superficially find those people irritating, in truth they serve as occasions for Mike to reassure himself that he is sensitive, intuitive, humble, trusting, peaceful, and free—or, if the occasion demands it, he can always find himself clear-headed, realistic, confident, reflective, assertive, and responsible.

Mike will also unwittingly manifest all four lists of qualities in his own behavior at various times. But, just as Ann called herself easygoing when, in truth, she was lazy, he will equivocate about his own qualities as well as the qualities of others. Try to be clear-headed with Mike, and he will think of you as cold. But when he is being cold, he will think of himself as clear-headed. And if anyone seems to encroach on Mike's cherished identity, that person will be relegated to the lower left list: someone who shows humility he will scorn as falsely modest.

The painful result of Mike's shrunken sense of self is that his relationships are merely functions of his ego, and he doesn't connect with people as more than ideas. Saddest of all, he only sees himself as an idea, and not the perceiver of that idea. Through the *matrika shakti*, Mike has become a prisoner, and lives at the mercy of his own creation. His list of qualities has become his range of choices. He is missing out on all the other qualities he fails to recognize in himself. As in the case of Ann, he will have to own all the qualities on all his lists to free himself from the prison-house of his private language, with its bogus definitions and misapplications.

A point to keep in mind is that the traits we are attached to and identify with are actually our "positive" traits, though rationally we might call them negative. Whatever qualities we cling to most we cling to precisely because we have come to believe that those qualities are essential—inseparable from life itself. Even a woman who thinks of herself as dishonest, mean, weak, and selfish believes that those qualities are actually who she is, and that if she gave them up, she would die. And she would—that is, her lower self would. The death of the lower self is crucial to spiritual growth. Whether our self-esteem is low or high, it is still just a set of ideas to which we are attached, and must be given up in the same manner as every other object.

We also have to understand that the qualities we see around us are those we ourselves have; if you can recognize a particular quality in someone you encounter, then it's also in you. Sooner or later, on the way to liberation, you will have to own, master and transcend that quality. We can also see the dichotomizing games of the lower mind almost every time we are introduced to someone. Both parties put their best foot forward, and that best foot is usually constructed from the qualities they identify as positive. Once we can see the qualities that make up another person's best foot, we can map out a full foursquare grid and have a much better sense of what to expect from all sides of that relationship. Of course, knowing someone else's lists avails us little if we aren't working constantly to own, master and transcend our own lists.

The foursquare game works because, being made in God's image, we have all qualities within us. In truth, we are pure Subject, containing and transcending all qualities, but through the *matrika shakti* we manufacture objective selves with which we then identify. We become all object, and then have to trace our way back to our original subjectivity. As we disentangle from the words with which we have constructed our lower selves, we gradually let go of our attachments and are free to act appropriately. Our consciousness moves back a step in the right direction. For a moment, we are then able to see that we are not a set of qualities but the ground of all qualities. When we finally liberate ourselves from identification with objects, no matter how subtle they are, we become who we truly were all along—the Self of All.

Chapter Eight
Stories of Baba, 1978

A Brahmin priest who had known Baba for many years often visited the ashram in Ganeshpuri. According to tradition, practicing Brahmins are vegetarians, and will not eat eggs. In the ashram, we observed the same practice.

Baba liked to cook, and one day for lunch he had helped make the *khir*, an Indian dessert. The Brahmin came to the back stair after the meal. I was, as usual, standing nearby.

"Did you like the *khir*?" Baba asked him.

"Yes. It was delicious."

"It had chocolate in it."

"Yes."

"The chocolate came from Switzerland."

"Oh, delicious," said the Brahmin. "Very good, very good."

"The chocolate had eggs in it," Baba said, and started laughing.

The Brahmin laughed along with him.

———— • • • ————

During the hot season of 1978 in Ganeshpuri, I was standing in the courtyard one day and an American man who had been sculpting statues of saints around the ashram approached Baba to ask what he should sculpt next.

As I stood in the back of the courtyard in the wilting heat, the image of a polar bear appeared in my mind. I said internally, "Polar bear, Baba. Polar bear." But I didn't make a sound.

Baba asked the man, "Where do they have all that oil?"

"Texas?" the man replied.

"No, the other place."

"Do you mean Alaska?"

"Yes. They have white bears there. Make a sculpture of one of the white bears they have in Alaska."

So I got my polar bear. Baba had listened to me inwardly and appreciated the joke.

———— • • • ————

Nothing really surprised anyone who spent time at the ashram. All sorts of things happened in the course of *sadhana*. During the hot season in 1978, I was standing in the courtyard and Baba was sitting on his long marble seat. Up the stairs from the lower garden came an Australian ashramite. But he wasn't on his feet. He was on his belly, slithering like a snake. His head was up, his arms at his sides.

The man actually moved like a snake, gliding across the courtyard in a manner I would never have expected from a human body. He slithered up to Baba's seat, bowed his head, and slithered away. Baba didn't even pay attention to him. No one thought it was particularly strange. When I saw the Australian later, his *kriya* (expression of *shakti*) had passed, and he was walking around normally.

———— • • • ————

The ashram in Ganeshpuri was in the jungle, and living in the jungle means constantly working to keep the wilderness at bay. Everything needed to be kept clean, or the jungle would move in quickly. Baba was emphatic about cleanliness.

Early one afternoon, he came out of his house, and he was "hot," as we used to say—angry and letting everyone know it. He held in his hand a stiff Indian broom, and he swung it around, declaring that the ashram was filthy and needed to be cleaned, that he had had it. Everyone was to get up and clean the place.

When Baba yelled, the vibration of his *shakti* went everywhere. Everyone immediately picked up whatever was handy and found something to clean. Amma, who loved documenting everything, came out with a tape recorder, handed it to me, pressed "record," and pushed me from behind toward Baba. Baba kept walking through the ashram, swinging the heavy broom and yelling, and Amma kept pushing me close to him, trying to get every word on tape. I expected him to turn on me, but he let us follow him around, getting scorched by the *shakti*. In a short while, the ashram literally sparkled; even the air looked and felt clean and full of energy.

When we checked the tape later, it was blank. Nothing had been recorded.

———— • • • ————

One morning in Ganeshpuri, shortly before lunch, I was in the front courtyard and Baba asked me to go find Damyanti. There were two ashramites named Damyanti, an American and an Indian, and it was clear that Baba wanted me to get the American Damyanti. I went looking for her but couldn't find her. Baba didn't seem to mind, and went inside for lunch.

After lunch, I took up my usual position by the back stair. When Baba came out a few minutes later, he looked at me and said, "Damyanti."

I found the American Damyanti in the dining room nearby and brought her to the back stair. When she arrived within a few feet of Baba, he said, "No! Not that one! No!"

Damyanti quickly left. I immediately went to retrieve the other Damyanti from where she was working in the kitchen.

Of course, Baba knew exactly what he was doing. I had to learn never to assume, always to check and be clear.

————— • • • —————

In August 1978, Baba was about to embark on his world tour. People were jockeying for position. Baba just sat and ignored the nonsense. A few of the corporate-minded men wanted a particular man to run the tour. He managed one of the big dorms for foreigners, and he and I were friends. Because we were close, I knew he was going through some things in his *sadhana* and was emotionally tenuous. That was normal; all of us had times when things were just hard internally.

I told Baba's translator that, for my friend's sake, he ought not to be put in charge of the tour. She passed on my concerns to Baba. When he spoke with the men, they responded that my friend was fine and that I had only questioned his fitness out of jealousy and that I wanted to be in charge of the tour. Baba played his role, appearing irritated with me. My friend agreed to manage the tour.

Everything went smoothly through Australia, Hawaii, and Oakland. Then we arrived in South Fallsburg, the biggest facility, and managing the large numbers of people coming and going became much more difficult. When we held a weekend intensive, it followed the usual pattern. In the morning, Baba would give *darshan* (public audience) and a talk, before giving everyone *shaktipat* during a long meditation. After a lunch break, the program was essentially repeated. It was hard work for Baba; he gave *shaktipat* to thousands of people at these events. After lunch, when it was time to start the afternoon program, my friend was nowhere to be found. At some point in the afternoon, a call came in. It was my friend. He was at the airport, about to board a plane for home. Much to my dismay, my fear had come true.

Now, of course, everyone knew I had been right, and they acknowledged it. Baba's translator reminded everyone of how I had tried to warn them. When, weeks later, my friend returned to the Fallsburg ashram, he quietly took care of himself, and never again entered the political fray. But he had the strength to come back. When confronted with something difficult, many people bolted, never to return.

———— • • • ————

When we first got to Australia, Baba stayed in a small house and had a modest evening program, but people always wanted to see him for private *darshans*. I had been assigned to handle those appointments. People would approach me to say they wanted to see him and I would jot down their names. I thought that anyone who wanted to sign up was supposed to get an appointment.

Baba grew angry with me for not having vetted them. "These people didn't need to see me privately," he said. "You're wasting my time."

Looking back, I can see why he was so angry. Most of the people wanted to ask Baba things that could have been addressed quickly and easily in the evening program. Those private darshans *were* a waste of his time. The point was to practice discernment, and know when a private meeting was needed, and when one wasn't.

———— • • • ————

In Hawaii in 1978, I lived a few houses down from the house where Baba was staying. It was gorgeous, and only a short walk from the ashram. But I found myself terrified. The terror came up for no reason, and everywhere I went I experienced the same feeling. I went to bed with terror, woke up with terror, and spent every moment of the day with terror. It never attached itself to any particular object; it just saturated my experience. No matter how much I sat with it, it wouldn't go away.

During that time, I started assisting with Baba's correspondence. One evening, I was in Baba's house, working with his translator. She had her own room there with its own shower, and a door passed directly from the shower to the outside so one could avoid tracking sand into the house. Baba was in his own room, and I assumed he didn't know I was there. It was late, and I probably should have been back in my own house. Suddenly, we heard Baba's voice in the living room, and we panicked. As far as I knew, Baba wasn't aware of all the work I was doing and wouldn't approve of my being there so late. We decided that I should slip out the shower door.

No sooner was I outside than Baba entered the room and started talking with his translator. The large, plate glass windows began only a couple of feet off the ground, so there was no way I could go any farther without Baba seeing me. I crouched down under one of the windows and, with my terror, waited. As I squatted there, a dog wandered through the bushes from a neighboring yard. The dog stood a couple of feet away and stared at me, and I stared back. The dog didn't bark. At that moment, the whole veil of illusion dropped away. I knew that Baba knew I was there, and that he knew I knew.

I had no terror at all, and everything was perfect. Everyone was a participant in the great play of perfection. Instead of the terror, I experienced pure bliss. Then I heard Baba leave the room.

As I walked home, the terror came back, but I now knew that it wasn't me. Instead of being identified with it, I could see it as an object, a vibration separate from me. If God wanted me to live with terror, then instead of running from it, I would accept it. I made it no big deal—just something to live with. By the time we left Hawaii a few weeks later, the terror was gone.

Chapter Nine
The Practice of Meditation

Meditation may be the most misunderstood part of spiritual practice. Nearly everyone has an idea about it, but few understand what it really is. In yogic terms, meditating is proceeding from concentration (*dharana*) to meditation (*dhyana*) to absorption (*samadhi*). Concentration is that primary ability to focus your attention on one thing. Meditation is sustained, one-pointed concentration. Absorption occurs when the meditator, the process of meditation, and the goal of meditation are revealed to be one. The final goal of meditation is liberation, which means becoming pure Subject.

Most of us already meditate without knowing it. We can only accomplish most things through sustained concentration, which is a kind of meditation, though outwardly focused. When we "lose ourselves" in an activity, we are meditating, with some success. Unfortunately, we are meditating in the wrong direction for spiritual practice. What we really want to do is lose our small selves in pure Consciousness. We become what we meditate on, so where we direct our attention is even more important than the act of concentrating itself.

All meditation is not equal. Like any other practice, meditation has to progress over time, through consistent hard work. You will have to refine and strengthen your skills of meditation in order to go deeper. A useful analogy here is baseball. Learning to meditate is like playing Little League; you learn to throw, catch, hit, and run. If you stick with the game, you will continue using the same skills but sharpen and strengthen them. High-school baseball requires more of you, and only those players who have the ability and discipline to keep honing their game will play in college or beyond. Even in the Major Leagues, the same skills are essential, and players constantly work on fundamentals even as they perform at the highest level.

Beginning meditation—the kind often taught at workshops and retreats—is simply learning how to concentrate. The focus may be on the breath, thoughts, emotions, or sensations in the body, but these objects of concentration are all superficial. There are benefits to this kind of concentration: people function more efficiently, handle stress better, and free themselves from distractedness. But those by-products are not the true goal. Above all, meditation is not a thought process, and it doesn't happen in the psychic instrument. True "mindfulness" is not sitting and watching your thoughts— who, after all, is doing the watching?

Concentration is the starting point. Most of us like to think of ourselves as being able to concentrate, but we actually spend most of our time distracted, racing from one thought-form to another. Examine your own mental activity for five minutes, and you will see a circus of distractions. Sitting and watching that chaotic activity will get you nowhere spiritually. If anything, you will become more agitated—and boredom is just one way of being agitated.

Once you've learned to concentrate, you will have to change the nature of your concentration. You will have to focus on more subtle objects, with subtler forms of attention. At this more refined level, the by-products change as well. You gain insight, suppleness of mind, more freedom from outer vehicles, and a greater sense of inward stability. But you will still be using the lower mind.

After a good deal of practice, you can reach the deepest levels of meditation. At this point, you let go of your small self and rest in the Heart. There isn't anyone to do *sadhana* anymore; there is only Consciousness. The deepest meditation is a state of perfect stillness and freedom.

To begin meditating, find a quiet place as free from external stimuli as possible. Adopt a comfortable posture that you can hold without strain for a long time. The only requirement is that your back remain straight and your head steady. You can sit on the floor or in a chair. You can kneel. You can even lie on your back, though lying down increases the risk of falling asleep when you want to stay conscious. Do not get caught up in the misguided pursuit of a variety of postures (*asanas*); the one *asana* to acquire is repose in the Heart. Some people believe they can keep their eyes open when they meditate. That is not the case for beginners; in fact, keeping your eyes open will encourage you to put your attention into your senses.

Once you have settled in, shift your attention and your intention inward, toward the center of your chest. At first, you will tend to find yourself back up in your head, listening to mental chatter. This is when you must resist the temptation to wrestle with your mind. Instead, keep bringing your attention down into your chest. This will feel like work—because it is work. In the same way that we have to drill in order to develop our athletic skills, we have to repeat the process of getting out of our heads again and again as we learn to meditate. You will have to train your will to stay out of your head. Until you do, your meditation will be more like bungee jumping than like settling into the depths.

At first, you may actually benefit from focusing on outward things like breathing or *mantra*, which are useful for learning concentration. As you go deeper in your practice of meditation, you may inwardly and silently repeat a *mantra*, letting go of the physical senses and redirecting and steadying your attention. But a *mantra* will only have real value if it is alive—that is, if it is filled with the vibration of what it designates. Only then will you go where it points you. And receiving a *mantra* from a teacher does not guarantee anything. It might have been alive when the teacher said it, but unless the disciple repeats it from the same depth, it will have little or no potency. Shallow, rote repetition of a *mantra* will have little effect.

There are four levels of speech to keep in mind here. The first is from the tongue—the most facile and shallow way to speak. The second is from the throat, which is deeper but still superficial. Only with the third level, from the Heart, do we speak from a place aligned with Truth. The fourth level, referred to as below the navel, is where sound originates.

But you must understand that the physical body, which is associated with the waking state, is merely an echo of the deeper vehicles: the subtle, causal, and supracausal bodies, which correspond respectively to sleep, deep sleep, and the unchanging Witness of the other outer three states. The path from one vehicle to another runs through the center of each body and to the Heart. You must work your way inward, piercing through the centers of subtler and subtler bodies, until you arrive in the Heart. Meditation, like the rest of spiritual practice, is about the Heart.

Learning to meditate also means learning to overcome the various obstacles to meditation. Our vehicles can disrupt our practice in a number of ways, and it helps to know the most common forms of distraction.

Physical Discomfort

The most obvious of these obstacles is physical discomfort. Working on your posture and flexibility in general will help you gain a steady meditation position. Though *hatha yoga* has little to do with the real business of spiritual practice, it can help you gain flexibility. If you are distracted by physical discomfort while meditating, the first remedy is to examine the source of the distraction. Is it a chronic issue, like a bad knee? If so, then consider sitting in a chair or even lying down; attachment to a position that isn't healthy for you is inappropriate. On the other hand, ordinary discomfort from holding a position can be relieved by two techniques. First, simply relax the area of discomfort, letting it settle into stillness. If that doesn't work, then practice withdrawing your attention underneath the discomfort. *Pratyahara*, the withdrawal of the senses into the Heart, will make the discomfort irrelevant. What you are doing is going deeper than the experience of physical pain or pleasure.

Mental Chatter

Mental chatter is a far more daunting obstacle than physical discomfort. While physical pain may distract us, mental chatter draws us into its sphere of activity. We get lost in it, and lose our capacity to reflect. Usually, we only shake off mental chatter when we get bored with it. Breaking out of it is a discipline unto itself. The key is not to resist mental chatter, but to redirect your attention to the Heart. If you try to wrestle with mental chatter, you will simply be meditating on mental chatter.

As a useful analogy, imagine yourself in a room with a blaring radio you can't turn off or even turn down. The only thing to do is leave the room. Your mind is like that radio. The way to still it is to leave it behind. When you do that, you stop feeding energy into your mental chatter. Just as a child throwing a tantrum will only calm down when it sees that no one is paying attention to its outbursts, the mind will eventually grow quiet if you stop fighting with it and just let it go. You don't still the mind by suppressing it. If it won't shut up no matter what you do, then go ahead and listen to it consciously for a few minutes, and it will get bored with your detachment. Accept where it is, then let the small self go.

Falling Asleep

Another common problem is falling asleep. If you are tired or depleted, as many of us often are, it can be difficult to stay awake once you close your eyes. It isn't unusual for my students to begin meditating, only to find themselves either slipping into dream state or waking up an hour later refreshed from a spell of deep sleep. Naps are wonderful, but they are not meditation. The point is to remain conscious while traversing whatever states you encounter. If you find yourself drifting off, don't get frustrated; simply resolve to stay conscious for as long as you can. As you meditate more, you will be able to stay conscious longer. Ultimately, you will go beyond sleep. If you can remain conscious and keep going in, at some point there will be a shift from individual consciousness to pure Consciousness.

Inner Experiences

When we do remain conscious in meditation, internal experiences, or the lack thereof, can take us off track so that we lose sight of our goal. Sometimes powerful experiences will arise in our consciousness; the lower self will attach to them. Such things as internal lights and sounds, to say nothing of more overwhelming experiences, can help draw you in, but they can also become occasions for pridefulness. It is vital to remember that they are simply signs ordinarily experienced along the way. When you start looking forward to having experiences, then you need to step back and remember the goal of spiritual practice.

On the other hand, the absence of striking inner experiences can be frustrating as well. It is tempting to regard a lack of fireworks as a lack of progress. This is not the case. There is actually no such thing as experiencing nothing. Just let yourself experience what you call "nothing," and you will find yourself moving and experiencing something. Inner experiences of any kind are nothing more than experiences. They are still manifested objects, and we should not give them more credence than they deserve. We have to remain one-pointed, as walkers intent on their destination take note of road signs and scenery but don't stop to revel in them.

Remember that as you walk further and further inward, you will find that absorption itself has many levels. The process grows increasingly subtle. You will have to pass through a number of stages before you reach the place of pure Subject with no object. Though these stages of absorption go by different names in different spiritual traditions, they are common to all of them. Even in pure surrender to God without progressive practice—what Patanjali calls *Ishvara pranidhana*—one plunges through these stages. Returning to God along this route through the Heart is our common destiny, but it takes time and commitment.

When you go into the Heart in meditation you have to remain there, which is a matter of will. Right effort here is, paradoxically, no effort. It takes effort to maintain our personalities, to cling to what we think we are; when we have left behind all our attachments and rest in the Heart, we exert no effort. The Heart, as the place of pure being, simply *is*. Remember, our goal is to trace back to pure Subject, the Perceiver; anything that can be perceived isn't the Self.

Above all, we have to remember that meditation doesn't end when we stand up. Spiritual practice is essentially a continuous meditation. If we meditate only in a perfect setting, or only when we set aside time for it, we will see some benefits, but we will not be resting in our essential being as a moment-to-moment practice. The question becomes: Can we carry our meditation with us? After sitting meditation, try remaining in the Heart while performing a simple physical action, such as picking up a box of tissues. Once you can do that, expand your meditation into other mundane activities, then into everything you do. Eventually, you will meditate constantly, regardless of your outward activities. Here, in *sahajsamadhi*, we look from the Heart out at the world. This is true meditation.

Chapter Ten
Stories of Baba, 1978-1979

While we were in Hawaii in the fall of 1978, I lived with several women in a house down the beach from Baba's. Staying with Baba in his house were his valet, his translator, her younger brother, and Amma. Baba's translator was then in her early twenties, a few years older than her brother. She liked to enjoy herself, and it was suggested that one evening, a bunch of us have dinner at our house. Her younger brother was the only male there. We made spaghetti and then relaxed in the yard. The two siblings pretended to be characters from a Bollywood movie, peeking and hiding among the palm trees.

After dark, they realized that they needed to get back to Baba's house. They asked me to escort them, thinking that, if I were with them, Baba would understand that nothing untoward had happened. When we reached the stretch of beach in front of Baba's house, we could see the whole back of the building. It was almost all plate glass, with sliding doors. The lights were out and the sheer curtains fully drawn. The brother was chosen to open the door, while his sister stood ten or fifteen feet back to the side and I stood several feet out from the door. It was locked.

The brother turned around in terror. Then, inside the house, a light went on. Just inside the door, sitting on a chair only a few inches from the glass, was Baba, lit from behind and staring out at us. He was not smiling.

All three of us panicked. Baba's valet opened the glass door, and Baba stepped out. He was furious. "How many boys were there?" he yelled at me. I told him there were no boys except for the translator's brother, and we had only eaten spaghetti and played in the back yard. I promised repeatedly that no other men had been there. Once he was satisfied, Baba stopped yelling and, after a while, he sent me home.

One of the lessons Baba taught me was how to be a good parent, which means being both a disciplinarian and a nurturer. He was, to me, both father and mother. He did it all, always with my best interest in mind. In this case, he played the role of the disciplinarian impeccably.

———— • • • ————

In the ashram, whenever I was left without a clear job and needed to sit and work through something, I would do seed cleaning. Seed cleaning meant sorting through spices on a metal tray and picking out rocks and sticks. It was silent work, no matter how many people were doing it. In America, it also meant peeling garlic and so forth. I would do it for two hours at a stretch. Sometimes it was blissful. Other times it was painful. It depended on my inner state.

The first time I did seed cleaning was in Hawaii in 1978. At that point, Baba was beginning his world tour, and politically minded people around me were jockeying for position. My responsibilities, which now included helping with Baba's correspondence, were limited, so I ended up doing seed cleaning every day. I was in the midst of the constant terror that had taken hold in my mind shortly after our arrival in Hawaii, and seed cleaning grounded me. It was a mundane job and therefore free of ashram politics, so no one bothered me. I would say a *mantra* and work quietly.

After Hawaii, I did seed cleaning in Oakland for one day. Baba was angry with me about something, so after he came to our chant one morning, I knew I needed to go right to the kitchen, put on an apron, and look busy. Shortly after I got there, someone came to the kitchen and said that Baba wanted to see me. I found him in the meditation hall and stood waiting, still in my apron. Amma was with him. Without realizing it, she had got wrong the name of a man who had written Baba a letter.

Using the name Amma had given him, Baba asked me who the man was. The man's name consisted of two first names, something like John Chris. Everyone was looking at me, and I could feel them rooting for me, because it was clear that this was a test.

"No, Baba," I replied. "It's Chris John. He's the chemist who was a whistle-blower and lost his job, and he was upset and asked for your help." I had passed the test, and everyone watching relaxed.

Baba gave me a wry smile. "What work do you do?"

"Kitchen, Baba." We all knew that, despite my apron, I didn't really work there. But it was the only right answer, because it was true at the moment and proved that I wasn't identified with any role.

He smiled again. "No. You can stay here."

That was when I officially became Baba's appointments secretary.

———— • ● • ————

Normally, no one ever said no to Baba. Most people always said what they thought would please him. But I was always forthright with him.

In Oakland, Baba had a study where he sometimes met with people. I happened to be in that room one day, and Baba turned to me.

"Do you want to give a talk in the evening program?" he asked.

It was customary for people to give talks about their experiences.

"No, Baba," I said.

Baba gave me a look of mock anger, so I continued. "If Baba wants me to give a talk in the evening program, I'll give a talk."

"Yes," he replied. I gave a talk a couple of weeks later.

Baba used my candor playfully, sometimes as a teaching tool. Years later, in Ganeshpuri, when I was a few months pregnant, I arranged to have the baby delivered in Bombay at Breach Candy Hospital. Baba, who knew of those plans, walked up to me in the courtyard with the head of Kaliyan Hospital in tow. At the time, Kaliyan was a crowded and unsanitary facility.

"So you're having the baby at Kaliyan," Baba said to me, knowing full well I wasn't going to have my baby there.

"No, Baba. You remember, I'm going to Breach Candy. I'm going into Bombay to have the baby."

I knew what Baba was doing. He was teaching the head of Kaliyan, and he knew he could count on me to see what he was up to and play a part in the lesson without trying to flatter him. In that moment, he and I enjoyed a shared performance.

———— • • • ————

While we were in Oakland in 1978, an older ashramite involved herself in some internal politics. She repeated a couple of gossipy things that caused problems. She was also extremely meek. One day, Baba called me to his study. This woman and Amma were there with him.

Baba stood there and yelled at me. He berated me fiercely for what the other woman had done. While he was doing it, I experienced bliss. The woman stood by, cringing, because she knew she had actually done the deed. In reality, Baba was yelling at me because she couldn't have handled being yelled at herself. I experienced the bliss of his *shakti* while she was actually scorched by her own guilt.

One thing was clear: If I was clean and free from attachment when Baba yelled, I experienced bliss. If I had any attachment, I was burned.

————— • • • —————

In Oakland in 1978, a couple who had left the ashram some time before turned up wanting a private meeting with Baba. They had lived in the ashram for many years and felt entitled to special treatment. Because I was Baba's appointments secretary, the woman came to me and asked me to arrange the private meeting. Baba told me he wouldn't see them privately, but that they could come to the evening program.

The woman wasted no time spreading word around the ashram that I, the gatekeeper, was running a power trip and had decided to keep them from seeing Baba. When the couple complained to Baba's translator, she said, "No. Rohini doesn't have the power to make that decision. Baba decided it." The couple had to face reality.

That sort of thing happened all the time in the ashram. People didn't want to see that Baba was there to teach them lessons they didn't always want to learn. I was often an unwelcome messenger, and had to get okay with that role.

————— • • • —————

"Big people" is what Baba would call the VIPs and celebrities who found their way to the ashram. Some were difficult, but many were sincere and easy to work with. One famous young actress got married by Baba. She wore my jewelry at her wedding. Though she was vibrant and self-assured on-screen, she was much less confident in person. On the other hand, when I had to spend a week in Ganeshpuri taking care of a world-famous pop singer with a reputation as a demanding diva, she proved to be friendly and unpretentious.

Show business types varied. Another well-known film actress and her husband were friendly, open, and no big deal, while a young British actor attending a program at the Palace of Fine Arts was so insistent on getting star treatment that I had to yell at him.

A famous Latin American actor was very nice, but his wife acted intolerably.

An opera tenor came at a low point in his career for counsel from Baba and left recharged, while a pop singer sang beautifully for Baba but seemed unable to keep herself from being defined by her sadness.

One of the most loved television actors of the time didn't even ask for an audience with Baba. He just quietly showed up for an evening program and sat with everyone else. One night, a few of us were invited to dinner at the house of a famed playwright and his actress wife. The husband was cold, the wife shrill and difficult.

But "big people" came from outside the entertainment world, too. A renowned expert in self-transformation proved one of the coldest people I have ever met.

A famous psychiatrist and his wife, both of whom seemed weird to me at the time, later admitted that they were stoned whenever they visited, as if anyone needed drugs to feel good around Baba.

A U. S. senator famous for his charity was genuine and kind.

A wealthy, aristocratic elderly gentleman, who owned an island, arrived with his wife at the Fallsburg ashram in an old Cadillac, wearing a pinky ring from Captain Kidd's treasure and just enjoyed himself, telling outrageous stories.

In Oakland, several former Black Panthers came for individual counsel with Baba. They were all gracious and sincere.

The "big people" were in reality no more or less confused than anyone else. In many cases, I had no idea who they were until after they left. The point was to respect their accomplishments and to see God in them as in anyone.

———— • • • ————

As a great guru, Baba was often visited by self-styled gurus. They came in all varieties. Baba had me take care of them.

An Indian guru from South Africa had recruited two of the top Transcendental Meditation people, and through them obtained that organization's internal British mailing list. Though he radiated a lot of *shakti*, to me he was unimpressive. He had nothing to offer beyond energy, and energy alone doesn't accomplish anything.

A young Indian woman—thin, long-haired, and clad in an orange *lunghi*—had a small entourage and no *shakti* at all. I didn't understand why anyone would follow her.

One visiting guru I really liked was a Brooklyn housewife high on *shakti*, who had been called an avatar by Ram Dass. She had no discipline and no sense of propriety, but she was outrageous and fun and attractive. She was also unpretentious, without a whiff of self-righteousness, and good at heart. It was easy to see why people felt good around her. She wouldn't take anyone very far, but she was fun. She went into her *darshan* with Baba wearing about twenty diamond studs in each ear. When she came out, they were gone. He had told her to take them off. She had no problem with that.

At one point, I got involved in negotiations with Da Free John, originally named Franklin Jones. He had experienced *shaktipat* while studying with Baba and decided he was fully realized. He left thinking of himself as Baba's equal and set up shop in California. When he returned to visit Baba, he expected a personal audience, a sort of guru summit. Baba said he could come to the evening program. Da Free John made all sorts of demands, including that his seat at the program be at the same height as Baba's. That was the sort of thing visiting guru types would argue about: where they would sit relative to Baba. When Da Free John didn't get what he wanted, he opted not to come at all.

A particularly interesting guru who visited Baba for a long while was Ma Yoga Shakti. She was an Australian witch. She was very strange, blonde, and a bit matronly. With her was a gaggle of adopted children, blonde and blue-eyed, who behaved exceedingly well because, it turned out, they had been given homeopathic opium. Despite her controlling personality, she could sense things, and once was able to recognize that I had had a powerful experience. She told me then that I was as close as I had ever been to nonduality, and she was right. But she couldn't offer anyone anything herself. She had some power, and was devoted to power, but power didn't make her happy, and Baba wanted us to see that. He was gracious to her in order to help her and also to help her adopted children, whom he showered with the love they didn't normally receive.

Many times, Baba showed his willingness to work with people, including these gurus, wherever they were, in order to teach them. In our ignorance, we sometimes failed to recognize what he was doing.

Baba also had me read things. He assigned me a book on Eckankar, for instance, and had me give him a report on what was right and wrong with it. I found it ridiculous and told him so. At best, the first part of an Eckankar sentence would be okay, but the second half would then be off by one or two degrees, which of course would send an aspirant way off track over time.

Baba was fond of saying, "Thank God for false gurus. How would we know the true gurus without the false ones?"

———— • • • ————

One visitor to South Fallsburg was the publisher of a glossy, eclectic magazine on spirituality that presented snippets of wisdom. He looked the part of the academic publisher: very tall, tweedy, and fitted with horn-rimmed glasses.

The man was exasperating. He habitually turned up unannounced, expecting immediate and privileged access to Baba. He even started soliciting financial support from ashramites, trying to build a sort of bloc within the ashram that would convince Baba to support the publisher's projects. More than once, he tried to bully me, threatening to report me to Baba if I didn't fit him into Baba's schedule or help him solicit funds around the ashram.

During weekend intensives, Baba never scheduled any private appointments. Regardless of this, the publisher called me a few days before an intensive and demanded a private meeting with Baba that Saturday. When I told him it was impossible, he declared that Baba would make room for him. I recommended to the publisher that he wait in the lobby. That way, if Baba wanted to speak with him, he would do so.

Saturday came, and the publisher positioned himself in the lobby with a coterie of his financial backers. When at last Baba walked by, the publisher stepped into his path and started to talk about his project. Baba brushed him aside, saying it wasn't the time for such discussions.

"But Rohini told me I could see you," the man whined. Baba was clearly annoyed.

While waiting to enter the hall, Baba sat down and called over one of the man's backers, a woman in a wheelchair. I followed and stood behind her without letting her notice me there. Baba asked her who had told them they could meet with him during an intensive, and she replied, "Rohini." I silently shook my head to indicate that it wasn't so. She left and, a few minutes later, while he was greeting people in the meditation hall, Baba loudly upbraided me for the alleged breach of protocol. I explained that the publisher had been harassing me for months, and told Baba exactly what I had in fact said to the publisher. Baba told me to go tell the publisher he was a pompous, insensitive, arrogant fool. I had no problem delivering that message. The publisher stormed off, shouting threats at me as he left. He immediately wrote a letter complaining that I was a poor representative of Baba.

For the next several days, whenever Baba and I went over his daily schedule, Baba said, "I'm going to get you." Through a third party, Baba invited the publisher to come to accept an apology, which, of course, was to come from me.

When the publisher arrived, I stood anxiously by Baba's door. The publisher gave me a look of gleeful scorn as he entered. Then Baba called me in. He sat there with the two of us a few feet apart in front of him. He berated me, calling me all kinds of names. I accepted the rebuke quietly, saying only, "Yes, Baba." When he was finished, Baba simply told me to leave. Through the whole ordeal, the publisher sat back and relished my humiliation.

As soon as I had left, Baba turned to the publisher. "Did you see how she handled herself?" he said. "That's what you should have done when she called you names. I told her to say those things to you. Now go out and apologize to her for your arrogant behavior."

———— • • • ————

One afternoon in Fallsburg, Baba called me up and asked me to look into something about an Indian swami who was staying at the ashram and report back what I found after the evening program.

I got the information and wanted to give his translator a heads-up because she always wanted to be in the know. All through the afternoon, I tried to get hold of her, but I couldn't get through. We sat next to each other, as usual, at the evening program, but no chance to speak with her arose.

After the program, I followed Baba out and said to her, "Would you please translate?"

She gave me a confused look but agreed. I gave Baba the information, and he and his translator left. Afterward, she wouldn't talk to me. I tried to discuss with her the ashram's next-day business, but she said, "I'm just a translator. You don't need to talk about this with me. You figure it out." What had been a shared responsibility was now mine alone.

The translator sulked for four days, refusing to talk to me. When she finally cooled down, she said, "I've never been this upset with anyone other than my mother." This worried me, because I loved her mother, and the translator treated her very badly.

It all blew over eventually, but it was a classic example of how the world remained in the ashram. I always felt that Baba set that one up. I was supposed to learn not to care what his translator, or anyone else, thought or said. And she was supposed to learn a lesson of her own.

———— • • • ————

Because of my work with Baba, I had many opportunities to see him in his private room. When I entered and looked at him, I could see that, inside, Baba was nothing and everything. I would watch him enliven, put on his mind and personality, and begin to speak. The effect was like watching lights gradually come on in a house. It was clear that he lived in infinity, and had to limit himself to function on the physical plane.

———— • • • ————

In Fallsburg in the summer of 1979, Baba gave me a wonderful gift. During an evening program, a woman brought him a beautiful five-string male tamboura. He turned, looked at me, and handed it to me.

"This will be good for you," he said. "It's good for the mind."

Even though, as Baba's appointments secretary, I sat close to him during evening programs, I was now required to stay close for a different purpose as well: to play that tamboura during the chant portion of the program.

Months later, the night after I lost my position as appointments secretary, I sat at the back of the hall during the evening program. I wanted to hide. Afterward, someone told me that I should have sat up front in order to play the tamboura. That reality, which Baba had made possible through his gift, hadn't occurred to me. Though I had become a nobody, Baba kept me nearby and involved, with a clear task to perform. He wasn't going to let me run away. His love was always there for each of us.

———— • • • ————

One time in Fallsburg, a woman came to visit her son, who was staying at the ashram. She was a cold, unfeeling person who wasn't at all interested in attending a program or seeing Baba. When she was about to leave, she said goodbye to me on her way out of the building.

I was standing outside the Namaste Room, where Baba held private meetings, and decided to make a courteous gesture. "Why don't you say 'Hi' to Baba before you leave?" I asked. "He should be out any minute." Baba was about to wrap up the day's last private *darshan*.

The woman waited in the lobby. The Namaste Room had no

view of the lobby. Where we were, there was no way Baba could see the woman was there. After the last private *darshan* ended and its participant left, Baba didn't come out. I told the woman to wait just a few minutes more, but he never appeared.

After fifteen minutes, the woman decided she had had enough, and left. At the precise moment that she walked out the front door of the building, Baba emerged from the door of the Namaste Room. He could not physically have seen her, but his timing was perfect.

———— • • • ————

One of the interesting things I did for Baba was find him teaching stories. He had me read the Gospel parables, Sufi stories, and the like, and suggest ones for him to read or use in his talks.

Baba wrote his books by hand in blue books. I would photocopy them and take them to his translator. Then I would help with the editing and proofreading of the translated text. I was in charge of compiling the index for *Where Are You Going?* The process was a great chance to study.

When I was no longer Baba's appointments secretary, I eventually worked in documentation. Every night, Baba's talk was recorded and transcribed. It was my job to make any corrections and give the talks titles so we could identify them easily.

Baba always gave people jobs that allowed them to learn. Whatever activity they needed, he provided. He didn't need me to do any of these things, but it helped me to do them.

———— • • • ————

Baba made lessons out of even the smallest tasks. He played

with us that way. In South Fallsburg in 1979, one of my jobs was to arrange private *darshans*. They took place at mid-morning in the Namaste Room, and involved as much time as Baba deemed necessary. He might give an answer in two seconds, or he might spend a half-hour or more with someone. I stood outside and directed people's coming and going. Inside, Baba would sit on a cushioned chair, with his translator on one side and an assistant on the other, sitting on the floor.

One day the assistant couldn't be there, and I was asked to cover part of her job. One of her tasks was to take Baba's slippers when he removed them, set them aside, and position them before him again when he left, the openings toward him, holding them so that he could slip into them easily. When he was about to leave, I placed the shoes down very carefully and stood by waiting for him. As he approached, Baba began laughing.

"You've never helped anyone put shoes on," he said.

I looked down, and the slippers were open toward me. It was mortifying. I knew I had put them down correctly, but somehow they had been reversed. I knelt and turned them around, and Baba put them on.

Chapter Eleven
Teacher, Student, Community

Spiritual practice is such a personal and interior experience that you might believe it has to be undertaken alone. That mindset is not only detrimental to the practice; it can be downright dangerous. In the first case, it will leave you with no external measure of your progress, or support in overcoming obstacles. In the second, it can tempt you to believe that you are special in your solitary quest for wisdom. If that delusion goes unchecked, you will stray further and further from God even as you believe you are getting closer. Only when you stop worshiping at your personal altar can you go far in spiritual practice. You need the guidance of a good teacher and the support of a practicing community to make that shift.

Another word for teacher is, of course, guru. Etymologically, the word is a combination of the Sanskrit *gu*, darkness, and *ru*, light. The guru takes students out of darkness and into light. In truth, the spiritual guru is not a person, but the grace-bestowing power of God, which dwells within each of us. A spiritual teacher is someone who has achieved a level of surrender that allows grace to operate through him and direct his students toward God. A teacher can guide you to the experience of your true nature. But how can you tell a true teacher from an ineffective or even false one?

A spiritual teacher has to have had a good teacher, so that there is a lineage of wisdom behind her. The master-disciple spiritual relationship that we now associate with the East was for ages an integral part of Western spiritual traditions, much like the master-apprentice relationship through which trade skills were passed on. But this principle of lineage and obedience, of received and transmitted wisdom, has largely been lost in the West. As long ago as the 10th century, St. Simeon lamented how third-level practice had been abandoned along with the sense of obedience to one's spiritual father. It is precisely that reverence toward the hard-won expertise of a legitimate spiritual director that is missing in contemporary society. People almost always look for the most qualified doctors, lawyers, or financial planners, but when it comes to spiritual practice, they seldom invest the time and care such a crucial commitment deserves. The teacher who makes you feel good about your lower self only cultivates the part of you that resists real spiritual practice. Where there is no rigor, there is no real teaching.

Many teachers claim to be part of a sacred lineage, but the trappings of a lineage do not make a teacher. A real tradition is passed on internally, so the fact that a teacher wears traditional robes or creates an environment that showcases her lineage doesn't indicate anything. Good teachers teach the essential Truth. They are not attached to externals, though they may have them around.

More immediately, you need to be clear about your own motives and goals in your search for a teacher. As my guru used to say, we get the teacher we want. If you carry a mental image of how a teacher is supposed to look and act, you may miss the best ones. Good teachers will not always look the part.

Truly accomplished spiritual teachers can both awaken and guide the spiritual energy of their students. A teacher who can awaken a student's *kundalini* but doesn't have the wisdom to direct that student toward the Self will do more harm than good. I once asked a *hatha yoga* instructor who talked a lot about spirituality what she would do if a student had a *kundalini* awakening in her class. She replied, "I'd dial 911." I'm not sure anything helpful would happen for her student in that scenario.

The most important indicator of a teacher's worth is how he interacts with his students. When you encounter a teacher, ask yourself a few questions as you observe his methods. Does he speak so as to connect with each student on a level deeper than intellect or emotion? A teacher who coddles students in order to create a feel-good experience for them may not have their best interests at heart. My Baba could be extraordinarily patient with his students, but he often said, "I give you what you want so that one day you will want what I have to give you." He could also be severe when appropriate. A good teacher affirms the true Self, not the personality, and helps students to let go of their attachment to what they thought was their true identity. Sometimes that guidance may take forms that at first appear harsh, but if followed to the end, lead to freedom and health—much as lancing a boil allows a sore to heal. This leads to another question: does the teacher foster dependency in students or lead them to freedom? A good teacher knows that her job is to help students become masters themselves, not to make them feel as though they would be lost without her guidance.

It often takes time to discern whether a teacher is appropriate for you. If, after several months in which you have obeyed a teacher's guidance, you do not feel as though your experience has changed for the better, then that teacher is not for you—though the teacher might be right for someone else.

That brings us to the role of the student. The student must be willing to learn or the whole endeavor is a waste of everyone's time. This means that the student has to face the rigors of spiritual practice and be willing to give up everything that isn't truly essential. Such surrender requires discernment. A student has to be able to trust that the teacher is coming from a place of wisdom and love, not seeking power and control. After all, a teacher can't "fix" a student; she can only give the student the tools of spiritual practice and help him recognize and seize opportunities to transform himself. Finally, the student must make a total commitment. Spiritual practice is not a lifestyle. It has to become the bottom line of your existence—not something you occasionally use to make yourself feel better, or something that props up your ego, or something that serves as an intellectual or emotional diversion. If you forget about the practice the moment you walk out of a session with your teacher, then you should reconsider your commitment.

There are many other ways to learn nothing from a good teacher. You can even live with a teacher for years and gain nothing if you don't want what the teacher has to offer. Some people are simply not equipped to grasp the subtleties of spiritual practice. Others lack the discipline to sustain their practice.

A common error is to buy into a false dichotomy that sets up spiritual growth against worldly success. The two are not at all mutually exclusive. After all, the practice is internal, and can be pursued regardless of your outward life. One of the most pernicious mistakes students make is relying on the teacher's energy and wisdom without imbibing the practice for themselves. Many people at Baba's ashram just basked in his *shakti* and never learned the practice. After he left his body, they were lost and confused, and either resorted to an empty, nostalgic lifestyle or gave up the spiritual life.

Ideally, your practice should involve not only sessions with your teacher but the community of other practitioners. We all need the support of others, especially those who share our commitment. Even the Desert Fathers of early Christianity met regularly to test and support each other's practice. Whatever other communities we belong to—family, civic, professional, social—only a spiritual community will offer us support in our practice as well as in our mundane activities. That support takes different forms. To begin with, we are often unreliable judges of our own spiritual progress, because the nature of the practice is that it goes right at our blind spots. Other students can help us uncover our ignorance, or provide empathy and encouragement as we go through the process of giving up attachments. Fellow students also offer each other practical support, both routinely and in times of crisis. We may undergo periods of relative solitude, but we are not meant to do this work alone.

At the root of teacher-student and student-student relationships is the need to keep good company. Good company is anyone or anything that encourages our health on every level. Apart from fellow practitioners, one form of good company is books, particularly scripture. Studying scripture can provide an intellectual framework for our experience and affirm the teachings of a true guru. A home environment that promotes stillness and harmony is an important part of spiritual practice as well. As we grow in our practice, we will learn how to be anywhere, in any company, without losing our way. Until then, we must choose our company wisely.

Baba used to say that God is everywhere, but until you can actually experience Reality all the time, it is healthier to be in a place of worship than in a bar. In ordinary life, our senses tend to be turned outward. A good teacher, community, and home environment work together to help us turn inward and find the Self.

Chapter Twelve
Stories of Baba, 1979

It was October of 1979, and I was no longer enjoying my job as Baba's appointments secretary. I was seeing more and more things I didn't like among the people who surrounded Baba. Too often, I had to deal with intrigues. Just as Baba always said, the world was in the ashram, just as it was everywhere else. I wanted out, but I didn't know any other way to be close to Baba.

Toward the end of the month, Baba's valet called to say that Baba wanted to meet me at his house. He was sitting in a dark room. In that darkness his brown eyes were brilliantly blue, and pierced right through me. Without once raising his voice, he spent over an hour quietly telling me how disappointed he was in me. He was able to list everything someone else close to him had done wrong—things I hadn't stopped from happening. This person had been indulged by people around her, and they concealed her secret activities from me, so I often had no way of knowing exactly what she was up to.

"You knew better," Baba said, "and you didn't stop her or say anything."

"I thought she was pure," I said.

Baba said that I was only digging myself in deeper by defending myself. In my lower mind, I thought how Baba had known what she was doing and hadn't stopped her, either. But that wasn't the point.

He was right. I had felt her secretiveness, and had never liked it. I should have learned to trust what I feel and speak up. Though I didn't realize it in the moment, Baba was freeing me by making me face what I had been unwilling to confront.

When he was finished, he said, "Okay, you can go now." I knew at that moment that my job was gone. I wouldn't be Baba's appointments secretary anymore.

That night, I had to do the evening program as usual. Later, I sat in my room. In the waking state, my eyes wide open, I experienced the complete dissolution of the physical universe.

The experience in and of itself did not last long. It was not meditative, but it was a breakthrough into Reality, both the dropping of a veil and the sense that a crack had opened in the physical plane, revealing what lies beyond. All the props that I normally called the world—walls, floors, lights, tables, even my body—dissolved. I saw both brilliant light and a luminous darkness. It was the void, it was the infinite, and it was all one. There was no lower self to grasp it. The experience didn't last long, but long enough to change everything. The "I" that I had been earlier in the day would never fully return.

By morning, I feared I might go crazy. The non-duality of that experience was hard for my lower mind to cope with. I was physically shaking, and very tenuous. But I knew from all I had been through in my *sadhana* that my task was to ground myself, and that the ashram *dharma* would help. I went to morning chant, and then went straight to the kitchen to do seed cleaning.

Somebody found me in the kitchen and told me that Baba had been looking for me everywhere for more than half an hour. I was taken to the main desk in what had once been the hotel lobby, and directed to pick up a phone. Baba was waiting at the other end of the line.

"Where were you?"

"I was working, Baba. In the kitchen."

"I did what I did because I had to. I love you. You are my daughter. Now forget everything."

I started sobbing.

"Where are you?" Baba asked.

"I'm in the lobby."

"Don't cry in public."

He hung up, and I went to my room and cried.

As months went by, the impression left by that experience of the void remained with me all the time. It was the background of everything I looked at. Living in its presence, I gradually recovered my ability to function efficiently. Ten years later, when I had the experience again, it was pure bliss.

———— • • • ————

Over the ensuing months, Baba took care of me behind the scenes, but in public he pretended he wasn't speaking to me at all. People were awful to me. They assumed that I had committed some terrible offense, though they didn't know what. From a worldly standpoint, I became a nobody. Through my practice, I had learned enough to know that I was working through a huge karmic lesson. I didn't defend myself, didn't tell anyone, didn't offer any stories. I knew that if I shared the experience I would diminish it and eventually lose it altogether. Instead, I disregarded what people thought of me and continued to practice what I had learned from Baba, boring inward and staying one-pointed on the Heart.

In November, Baba stayed at the ashram in Boston. The weather was cold and gray, the leaves had turned, and the rooms in the ashram were cold.

I was standing alone by the window of an unoccupied room in the ashram—nothing but bunks and cold bare floors. In front of the window was a tall space heater that had never been turned on. The room was cold. Baba walked in and stood silently beside me, both of us looking out the window. After a while, he put his arm around me.

"Hot, isn't it?" he said.

"Yes, Baba," I replied. "Hot."

There we were, standing by a cold space heater in a cold room in a cold city, but Baba knew that inside I was cooking. A few silent minutes later, he walked out, but he had gently let me know that he knew what I was going through and would continue to care for me as the karmic drama around and within me played itself out.

———— • • • ————

In Boston, during my outcast period, Baba told a story I felt was meant for me. Ten men planned to go on a pilgrimage to a holy site. On reaching their destination, one of them suggested that they take a vow to drink no *todi* (an alcoholic drink) and eat no fish while on the return portion of their pilgrimage, and his companions agreed. They all took the vow. On their way home, they grew hungry and stopped at a village for food. It was a fishing village, and the only food available was fish.

One of the men said, "Well, we should get some fish."

"But we swore not to," said another.

"Don't worry. No one will know." Nine of them enjoyed some fish, but the one refrained.

As they walked farther, they grew thirsty. Passing through another village, they found that the only drink available was *todi*.

"Let's have a drink," said one of the pilgrims.

The man who had declined the fish said, "But we took a vow."

The reply was the same. "Oh, no one will know." So all but the one man drank some *todi*.

When they returned to their village, one of the men said, "We took a vow not to eat fish and not to drink *todi*." Then he pointed at the one man who had honored the vow. "But this one man did both."

That was the end of the story. When Baba finished, he looked around the room and then at me, and said, "The truth prevails, but the majority always wins."

———— • • • ————

When we traveled from Boston to Miami in 1979, I had no role and was actively ignored. Though I normally left the airport with Baba as part of his entourage, this time I was told to stay at the airport with another ashramite and take care of Baba's luggage. That meant seeing to a few other people's bags as well—some 30 pieces of luggage for a 100-pound woman to carry. I rode in a truck with the bags. It was a symbolic demotion. I didn't fight it. Instead, I simply sat with the experience and witnessed it.

By the time I got to the Miami ashram, the festivities were over and everyone had dispersed. I quietly took in all the luggage, then found my room and began to settle in. Someone called my room to say there was going to be a press conference and I was needed to organize it. The same people who had thrown me in with the luggage now needed my help. "It's not my job anymore," I said. "There's someone else who does this." Then I hung up. They called back and said that the new person wasn't sure how to do it. That was the way it worked at the ashram; you got a new job and had to learn on the fly, because it wasn't really about the job.

After a while, a call came that settled the situation: "Baba wants you to come." I replied that I needed to iron some clothes and then would take care of the press conference. I had learned to accept whatever responsibilities came my way, without attachment.

Chapter Thirteen

Action in the World: Love, Compassion, and Empathy

Spiritual practice does not stop when your mundane life calls you to action. Your practice should inform not only what you do, but also how you do it—or, more precisely, the place within yourself from which you do it. As you go deeper within yourself and let go of your wrong understanding, your outward words and actions will be truer expressions of who you really are. Appropriate action, then, is action from a place of non-attachment—which means, among other things, not being attached to outcomes.

This brings us to *karma yoga*, the yoga of action. Its essence is selfless service: giving up the fruits of our actions to God. When we rest in the Heart, all our actions arise from God, and the lower self, with all its ambitions and ideals, is removed from the process. Rather than engage in behavior modification, which only deals with our outward surface, we need to go to our source to have our actions be Real. Unless we are fully realized, any action, no matter how good it may seem, is clouded by personal perception. Good works done from the wrong place are not wholly good. If you volunteer at a soup kitchen so you can think of yourself as a good person, then you are prideful, regardless of how good the action looks.

If, on the other hand, you volunteer at a soup kitchen because it is a fitting action, and you remain non-attached to praise, blame, or results, then you are practicing *karma yoga*. You must acquire the ability to be appropriate at all times, which can only occur when you are in harmony with the universe. This harmony is what the Taoist sages meant by the term *wu-wei*: not a passive, "go with the flow" carelessness, but a total surrender to the Self, so that our every action is an undistorted expression of Reality.

And because Reality is Love, everything done from the Self is an expression of Love. Absolute Love is pure bliss—the acceptance of everything as perfect just the way it is. It includes everyone and everything at all times. Even in our ignorance, it trickles down and manifests itself in small amounts in our lives. But the lower self, with its shrunken understanding, limits Love, only looking to make things better for itself. When we are no longer veiled, Real Love will inform all that we do.

Compassion is love with detachment, and such love doesn't always conform to the lower self's idea of love. Rebuking someone, for instance, is often seen as unloving and uncaring. When a person who is resting in his true nature of Love speaks sternly, his words will be compassionate and appropriate, whether the recipient recognizes it or not. Because he is Love by nature, all he does is motivated by Love. I once heard that Baba yelled at a young woman in the ashram in India, telling her to get out of the ashram by the next night. The following evening, she was still there. When people asked her why she hadn't left, she replied that Baba had been yelling at her ego, and it had left. She understood what lay behind his words.

Baba listened so deeply within himself that he could hear what was best for that young woman. Only by going deep within yourself can you truly empathize with someone else. Superficial commonalities and nice ideas about "oneness" only connect lower selves with other lower selves. In this respect, we function like wells. If we live at the surface of the well, we are each an individual, living a distinct life with our own interests, wants, and needs, separate from everyone else. If we begin the process of going down into the well, we may appear alone and even more separate, maybe even self-centered, for a while. However, when we go far enough down the well, we reach the groundwater, the true Self, which is everyone. In this place, "I" is everyone. We are no longer separate from others. There is no possibility of selfishness. We feel what others feel without the lower self inserting itself into the situation.

So practicing selfless service is loving your neighbor as the Self because you are your neighbor. This does not mean that what is good for you as an individual is good for your neighbor; it means that you will listen deeply and discern what is appropriate. What connects us is the groundwater. Once you have established yourself in the groundwater, service to all becomes a way of life. Selfless from the head is always selfish; Selfish from the Heart is truly selfless.

The non-attachment with which we practice real service allows us to discern what is really supportive in a given situation. Our culture encourages us to forgive and forget, and we are led to believe that being supportive means making someone feel good about his lower self, regardless of what he has done. But those habits can be destructive. Enabling your neighbor who has done injury to herself or others is not serving the Self in you or in your neighbor. Forgiving just to forgive is not helpful to anyone. There must be reflection, repentance, change, and turning around, before there can be forgiveness. We should want what, in truth, is best, not what is best for our neighbor's lower self. Because our true nature is Love, we would not want to injure ourselves, or anything or anyone else. And because all is "we," we would empathize with all. Yet sometimes our neighbor's lower self must be rebuked so that the Self can be uncovered for her. We must listen and act appropriately, consciously, and for the betterment of all. This is the real practice of non-injury: not the lower self playing nice, but the response of the Self to the Self. We let go of our individuality in order to feel what others feel.

In this context, we have to remember that letting go of our individuality does not mean going unconscious. Most people think that, if they were to give up their individuality, they would either be unconscious or a slave to others because they would no longer take care of themselves. In truth, we must give up our lower self, so that we are no longer unconscious or self-conscious but truly conscious. We are truly able to listen, love, care, and empathize with everything and anyone, including ourselves. The love of the lower self is a shadow of Love; the Self is All, All is loved, and All is considered and taken care of appropriately.

Chapter Fourteen
Stories of Baba, 1979-1981

In late November of 1979, we arrived in Miami and rented a hotel on the beach. I was still in the midst of being shunned by everyone for having supposedly committed an unknown but grievous offense to Baba. I was a nobody. I had no power and no role. I was no longer on call. I was left with nothing to prop up my lower self. One day, I decided to spend my free time going for a walk on the beach. Though it may seem insignificant, it was my way of declaring independence.

When I returned to my room, I started to get a headache, then nausea. I decided that no one cared whether I went to the evening program or not, so I chose to accept that I didn't feel well and not attend. Before, I would have gone to my job regardless; now, I could choose to stay in my room and sulk.

In the morning, I didn't feel any better, so I skipped the Guru Gita chant. Nursie, the ashramite who worked as Baba's nurse, noticed that I wasn't at the chant and came up to my room afterward. She checked me out and determined that I had sunstroke. When she asked if I wanted anything to eat, I asked for a banana and a bagel.

As soon as Nursie left to get my food, into my room walked Baba. He came to my bed, and I gave him the pouty look of a sick little girl. He put his hand on my forehead, as a mother would, looked into my eyes with love, and said, "I'll be right back." Before Nursie returned, he was back with sliced raw onions on a paper towel. "This will cool you down," he said, and watched as I ate them. When Nursie returned with the bagel and the banana, Baba said, "You can have the banana. Nursie can have the bagel." Nursie was thrilled.

Baba took charge of me for the rest of that day. He returned to my room every hour to check on me, feeling my forehead and asking me how I was doing. It was clear that he wasn't angry with me, and that he loved me and would take care of me. I had deluded myself into thinking that no one cared and that my act of defiance was actually going to free me. Baba showed once more that he cared about what was best for me, not about what I could supposedly do for him.

———— • • • ————

In Miami during the winter of 1980, I stayed in a room on Baba's floor of the hotel we had rented. Baba walked up and down the hall. We kept our doors open so he could come in and talk with us. One day I was sitting in my room when the phone rang. It was Baba. While serving as his appointments secretary, I had spoken with him on the phone every day, usually with other people on the line as well. This call was different. It was Baba alone, asking for a phone number, just as anyone else might. But around him, I always experienced expanded consciousness. This was a realized being calling me.

"Rohini?"

"Yes, Baba."

"Do you have [the person]'s phone number?"

"Sure. Hold on. Let me go get it." There I was, responding to a living saint in a completely ordinary way.

"Noni's coming," Baba said. "I'll call you back." He hung up. Clearly, he wanted the call to stay between the two of us.

When he called back in a few minutes, I gave him the information. He thanked me and hung up.

This was just a simple exchange between Baba and me, with no one else involved. I was able to have a completely mundane moment with him, but every such experience with him was heightened and full of life, full of his vibrancy. That experience of being with God in the midst of the ordinary was what I had come to Baba for in the first place.

———— • • • ————

During that stay in Miami, Baba knew things had been rough for me. One day he came into my room, held up his *mala*, looked intently into my eyes, and started saying, "*Guru om, guru om, guru om*," counting the beads of his *mala* one by one. He was giving me a *mantra*. He said it from the innermost place, where he lived, and he was teaching me to say it from the same place. Baba was giving me the means to overcome my wrong understanding in that difficult period.

By the end of that winter, I had reached a point where I was more or less at peace. I had reaped the resentment of many at the ashram, and quite a few ashramites were thrilled to see what they assumed was my fall from grace. But what Baba had really done was liberate me from the politicking that surrounded him. Baba had saved my life, no differently than he had when I had nearly died from malaria.

———— • • • ————

Baba used to celebrate the birthdays of devotees. In Ganesh-puri, people would approach him and say, "Baba, it's my birthday," and he would give them a scarf or similar token to acknowledge the event. On his world tour, he decided to make the birthday process more organized. I was assigned to arrange birthday *darshans*. People would sign up with me in advance, and before *darshan*, the birthday people would be called up from the back of the hall. They would *pranam* in front of Baba, and he would give them a gift and put a piece of candy in their mouths. It was all a bit silly, and I hated the job, but it was one of my responsibilities. In 1979, when I lost my job, the one thing I liked about my new status as a nobody was that I no longer had the birthday job.

In the summer of 1980, before we left for Santa Monica, Baba said that he liked the way I handled birthdays better than anyone else. Of course, he knew what he was doing. By the time we arrived in Santa Monica, I was handling birthdays again. When we were about to leave Santa Monica, there was a flood of calls from people whose birthdays were in a few days, all requesting that their birthdays be recognized at *darshan* on our last night there. The list grew to nearly twenty people, and I knew Baba would be angry. He had a huge number of people coming to that last evening program to say goodbye.

At the program, I called all the birthday people up, one behind another. After a while, Baba got angry and started yelling at me in Hindi even as he handed out gifts and put candy in waiting mouths. He was no longer smiling at the birthday people. By the time the last person came up, Baba was exasperated.

Afterward, I was relieved of responsibility for birthdays. I had, in effect, won my freedom from the job by doing exactly what I had been asked to do. And Baba never organized birthday celebrations the same way again.

———— • ● • ————

In Santa Monica in 1981, a prominent psychologist came to see Baba. He was known as a great humanist and a champion of unconditional love. Baba asked me to take care of this visit. I had learned over the years how to play by ear whatever Baba wanted, so even though I was no longer Baba's appointments secretary, taking care of this visitor wasn't a problem for me.

The ashram, a former motel, consisted of several buildings. Guests would be greeted at one building, and Baba would hold private meetings at another one a short walk away. The psychologist had scheduled a time for the meeting, so I introduced myself and talked with him, waiting for Baba to become available. At the appointed time, I escorted the psychologist to the other building, but I was told at the door that Baba wasn't ready. We went back to the first building and waited.

Three more times I walked the psychologist to the other building. Each time we were told that Baba wasn't ready. Only when the psychologist had completely lost his patience did word come that Baba was ready to see him. I had spent an hour apologizing for the long wait, and the psychologist—the same one who had written so influentially about unconditional love and being open to the moment—had grown more and more livid.

It was clear that Baba had set him up. Once the psychologist was angry, Baba could prick that anger in the meeting and free the man of it. Baba was always willing to teach that way.

———— • ● • ————

Over the years, Baba gave me several precious stones. A couple were citrines, which were nice but were not the guru stone —a yellow sapphire like the one Baba wore.

During Christmas of 1980, at the Santa Monica ashram, I was

proofreading transcriptions of Baba's talks and managing birthdays and odd tasks. Though I didn't talk with Baba's translator much anymore, I felt obligated to get her a Christmas present. When I brought it to her room Christmas afternoon, she was with her group of friends. She accepted the present indifferently.

I felt hurt and angry. As I walked back to my room, I said inwardly, "I'm done. It's over." I knew that I was through with that relationship.

Within fifteen minutes, I got a phone call requesting that I come to Baba's room. Baba was resting on his bed, and his translator was sitting nearby. Baba looked at me, and handed me something folded up in paper.

"Now you have the real guru," he said.

I opened it up, and it was an 11-carat yellow sapphire, the guru stone.

Baba and I knew the significance of that gift. He was telling me that I was free of the distractions surrounding him, and could just focus on God.

I still wear that sapphire every day.

———— • ● • ————

Once when I was wrestling with a question, I scheduled a private meeting with Baba in Fallsburg. I asked him, "How do I deal with apparent injustice?" I didn't trust my perceptions or my reactions.

"First," Baba said, "reach a place of dispassion. If you can't do that, then speak out—not with the expectation that anything will change, but for the sake of relieving your own heart."

———— • ● • ————

In 1981, in South Fallsburg, I went to see Baba privately because I was confused about some things I had seen going on at the ashram. Many of the political types at the ashram, those who had been around for a while and whom Baba called "old shoes," were constantly involved in intrigues about who would control what. Even when I was no longer head of security, I would see things that didn't seem right. I had learned to trust my sense of things and hide nothing from Baba. Because it wasn't always safe to tell him with other people present, I would look at his photograph in private and tell him internally what I had seen. At the evening program or elsewhere, he would look at me and nod his head knowingly, and whatever I had told him about would be dealt with.

At the private meeting, I asked him, "Aren't we all trying to get to God?"

"You're so naïve," he replied. "You think everybody's here for spiritual practice. There are very few people here for spiritual practice. Most people are here to hide, to escape, to run away, to find a husband or wife, to network for business, whatever. The world is here just as it is everywhere else."

I always felt bad for Baba because of that, but he was completely non-attached, and none of it troubled him.

That conversation reminded me of a story Baba once told about the abbot of a great monastery. When a visitor arrived, he saw hundreds of monks going about their monastic duties. He was astonished, and asked the abbot, "How many disciples do you have?"

"Two," replied the abbot.

Chapter Fifteen

A Companion to the *Yoga Sutras* of Patanjali

There is only one road home, but every great faith tradition has its own map, with its own legend and its own set of names. One of the oldest and clearest maps is that of classical yoga, also known as *raja yoga*, which is laid out in Patanjali's *Yoga Sutras*. Though scholars debate the date and authorship of the *Sutras*, the important point is that they work. If you find that Patanjali's approach doesn't suit your temperament, there are plenty of other good maps to choose from.

Making the *Yoga Sutras* accessible without being superficial isn't easy. The nature of the sutra form is to be as condensed as possible, which means that you can't comprehend sutras without expert guidance and careful study. Keeping that difficulty in mind, I've chosen to present an overview of the *Yoga Sutras* by laying out their essential principles. You will have to raise your game a bit to follow the subtleties Patanjali presents. Don't be afraid of the Sanskrit terms; they are all explained in context.

A Definition of Yoga

The word "yoga" has become commonplace. Mostly, it calls up images of people contorting their bodies on mats, even in rooms as hot as saunas, trying to achieve strength, beauty, and relaxation.

But physical training has almost nothing to do with true yoga. Feeling physically fit and relaxed is not being spiritual. The varieties of "yoga" taught in most classes nowadays may be sold as internal and spiritual, but they merely indulge the five senses. What these classes promote is personal power, beautiful bodies, and "healthy" lifestyles.

Many so-called yoga teachers talk in terms of "the mind-body-spirit connection" without knowing what that really means. The three entities are presented as somehow equal. If by "spirit," these people mean *prana shakti*, then the connection is valid: three vehicles used by the Self. But if by "spirit," they mean the Self, then they have no understanding of the Self, and no real understanding of yoga. The Self is Real. The mind and body are temporary and serve the Self.

Centuries ago, *hatha yoga* was developed as a way to purify the body. It was intended as a preliminary discipline, after which a person would be prepared to practice internal yoga. Over time, *hatha yoga* has developed into a complicated series of poses, or *asanas*, which have mistakenly become ends in themselves. There is nothing wrong with temporarily calming the mind and body, but this sort of work only sets the stage for true yoga, which requires going much deeper within.

In sutra 1.2, Patanjali defines yoga: *yogash chitta-vritti-nirodhah*. Translated from Sanskrit, this means that yoga is "the inhibition of the modifications of the field of consciousness." *Chitta* is the medium or field of consciousness. *Vrittis* modify the *chitta*. On their subtlest level, they are vibrations; on the gross level, they are feelings, thoughts, and words. As I explained in Chapter Five, a seed is a *vritti* that sets the field of consciousness vibrating. *Nirodha* is the inhibiting and stilling of these vibrations. This means that all vibrations, no matter how subtle, are to be stilled. The process of accomplishing this is the practice of yoga.

It is crucial that we understand that *chitta* does not mean "mind" in the usual sense. It is the medium through which *vrittis* travel from their source at the origin of all manifestation. Some people translate *chitta* as "mind," and then beginners see "mind" as just their own "chatter." This understanding can serve as a starting point, but the *vrittis* encompass much more than our mental noise. They are all the vibrations that manifest in the field of consciousness.

Patanjali defines the goal of yoga in his third sutra, which explains that we end by resting in our true nature—the Seer or pure Subject. The Seer is the Self, the Subject of All. It is pure Perceiver and cannot be perceived. It is both immanent and transcendent, both still and active, both manifest and unmanifest. It is Love itself, Truth itself, Consciousness itself. Until we have achieved stillness (*nirodha*), we are subject to the condition described by Patanjali in the fourth sutra: the Seer appears to be the modifications in the field of Consciousness (*chitta*).

In other words, unless we are resting in our true nature and enlivening our vehicles from there, we will believe that we are the modifications we should be stilling. The thought form "I am tall" is not true. My body, a vehicle, may be tall, but I would have to identify with my body in order to believe that "I am tall."

This is just one example of living in ignorance—taking what is not true to be true. As we still our vibrations, we will see that we are none of our vehicles: not our bodies, not our senses, not our minds, not our thoughts, not our feelings, not our personalities, not our experiences, not our energy. These are temporary things we use to function in the manifested world. We can perceive them, so they cannot be our true nature. As we gradually disentangle from who we are not, we achieve more stillness and the Self shines forth more clearly.

The Eight Limbs of Yoga

Turning inward means working from the outside in. Patanjali affirms this in his presentation of the eight limbs of yoga in sutra 2.29. The eight limbs form a progression.

1. Restraints (*yamas*)

2. Observances (*niyamas*)

3. Posture (*asana*)

4. Control of vital energy (*pranayama*)

5. Withdrawal of the outward senses (*pratyahara*)

6. Fixed concentration (*dharana*)

7. Meditation (*dhyana*)

8. Absorption (*samadhi*)

The *yamas* and *niyamas, asana, pranayama,* and *pratyahara* are all external limbs, or ways of purifying our outer vehicles so that the subtler internal work can be done. The three internal practices of *dharana, dhyana,* and *samadhi* form a progression that leads us toward the Self. As we will discuss later in more detail, even *samadhi* contains degrees of increasing subtlety.

Everyone starts with character building: we must learn to restrain ourselves externally before we can still our consciousness internally. The *yamas* and *niyamas* are simply the moral restraints and observances that we should all exercise in our lives. The Ten Commandments, for instance, are mostly *yamas.* Patanjali sets boundaries on human behavior that are almost universally accepted if not always followed: not injuring, not being dishonest, not stealing, not giving rein to desires, and not being possessive.

The *niyamas* are all moral qualities to cultivate: purity, contentment, self-discipline, self-examination, and devotion to God. While all these practices are good in themselves, in yoga they are meant to still the outer vehicles. They help eliminate the distraction and agitation that arise from an undisciplined character. The important thing to realize here is that character building is not about being "good" but about stilling everything that obscures the Self.

Calming our character is one thing; being able to sit still is another. In sutra 2.46, Patanjali defines *asana* as a stable and easy posture. Notice how this does not mean tying your body in knots or practicing a variety of postures. The one traditional absolute of *asana* is a straight spine. Apart from that rule, you should adjust according to the needs of your body and find a comfortable position. The point is to still the vibrations of the body, so you can turn inward and meditate for long periods of time without being distracted by that vehicle.

Once we have calmed the physical body, we can move to the vital energy that circulates through it. This energy is called *prana*, and it should not be confused with the breath; it is actually what is known in Chinese traditions as *chi*. Though *prana* "rides" the breath in its circulation, it is subtler. Sutra 2.49 establishes that once sound posture is achieved, we can suspend the flow of inhalation and exhalation—in other words, we can separate our *prana* from our breathing and still both.

The last of the outer limbs of yoga is *pratyahara*. Patanjali defines this practice in sutra 2.54: *Pratyahara* is the withdrawal of attention, by the mind and then the senses, from all outward objects. If you withdraw your attention from your five senses, they will turn inward along with your attention and no longer distract you by reacting to external stimuli. The often-used analogy of a turtle withdrawing into its shell provides a sense of how we disentangle from the outside world as we ready ourselves for the practice of deep meditation.

The first internal limb of yoga is *dharana*, or concentration, defined by Patanjali in sutra 3.1 as fixing the mind on one point. Nearly all of us are capable of concentrating in a limited way; we have had to discipline our minds to focus on one thing in order to complete most tasks. Everything from changing a tire to writing a memo requires fixed attention. That sort of concentration is largely unconscious, because we don't recognize it as a skill. In yoga, everything you do, both externally and internally, must be conscious. As you go inward, you must deliberately choose to redirect your awareness toward your true nature.

What many people think of as "mindfulness" isn't. True mindfulness is being conscious of what is Real and what is not. Simply being aware of your thoughts, or being "in the moment" emotionally, is only being conscious of what isn't Real. You can't be truly mindful while being *in* your mind.

Once we have consciously directed and focused our awareness, we must be able to sustain that one-pointedness. This practice is *dhyana,* or meditation, defined by Patanjali in sutra 3.2 as maintaining an unvarying flow of one-pointed awareness toward a chosen object. When we remain totally focused on one object for an extended period of time, we can reach a state in which the meditator, the process of meditation, and the object of meditation become one. This is *samadhi.*

Samadhi is what happens when the consciousness of the object is all that appears to exist. Patanjali defines *samadhi* in sutra 3.3: when the object of meditation shines forth as if your own nature is empty, this state is called *samadhi.* In *samadhi,* you are well beyond the unconscious activity and self-conscious thinking that dominate normal life. The lower self is out of the way and the object of your meditation shines alone.

Samadhi

The word *samadhi* is thrown around quite a bit in pop culture. Many people believe that any extraordinary experience that makes them feel totally absorbed and uplifted is *samadhi.* This definition suggests a sense of being unconscious and lost in something. But *samadhi* is not being lost or unconscious. It is a conscious state, not a form of oblivion. How sad it would be to think that the goal of spiritual practice is unconsciousness or nonexistence! Even as we practice and become more conscious and clear, this delusion lingers in the background, unnoticed yet impacting all. As you will see, it is what Patanjali calls *abhinivesha*, or clinging to the life of the lower self, and it leads us to believe that self-surrender is a leap into nonexistence. In truth, what we leave behind is our wrong identification, our shrunken sense of self, which keeps us unconscious or self-conscious.

In the *Yoga Sutras*, Patanjali reveals *samadhi* to be a process composed of stages in which we dive deeper and deeper into our own consciousness. And not all *samadhi* is spiritual practice; its more superficial forms may not have God as their object.

There are two fundamental kinds of samadhi: *sabija samadhi* and *nirbija samadhi*. *Nirbija,* or seedless, *samadhi* is only achieved at the point of liberation. Every prior stage of *samadhi* is *sabija samadhi,* or *samadhi* with seed; it contains some seed object, concrete or subtle, on which we focus our attention—some content in the mind. *Sabija samadhi* breaks down into two categories: *samprajnata samadhi* and *asamprajnata samadhi.*

Samprajnata samadhi, according to sutra 1.17, is *samadhi* with a seed object based on the senses (*vitarka*), reflection (*vichara*), bliss (*ananda*), or pure I-awareness (*asmita*): you choose a seed object upon which to fix your attention. As we will see, you move gradually from *vitarka* to *asmita* as you go deeper into *samadhi,* changing the seed at each stage. *Asamprajnata samadhi* is what happens when you move from one of those four stages to another. You let go of one seed object and, as your attention shifts inward to a deeper seed object, you pass through a temporary emptiness, a sort of cloud, which fills the mind during the transition from one stage of *samadhi* to the next. It is rather like leaping from one stone to another to cross a stream. For a moment, you remain suspended in the emptiness between two stages.

Asamprajnata samadhi does offer a momentary opening to *nirbija samadhi,* if you are conscious enough to seize it by completely letting go. For all but a very few, that is far too difficult. It is much more likely that you will have to progress through the four basic stages of increasing subtlety in *samprajnata samadhi,* working from the gross outer level to the subtlest Reality. Think of the differences as walking through a series of different environments, each of which is more free. Walking through molasses would be nearly impossible; through water, difficult; through air, easy. The reason it gets easier as you go is that you shed limitations.

The first layer of *samadhi* is *vitarka samadhi.* It focuses on something perceived by the senses as its seed object. If you concentrate all your attention on a candle and hold it there until there is no content in your mind other than that candle, then you are doing *vitarka samadhi.* But it's more complicated than that. *Vitarka samadhi* breaks down into two layers: *savitarka samadhi* and *nirvitarka samadhi.* Sutra 1.42 defines *savitarka samadhi:* in this state, the name, form, and meaning of the object of concentration are held together in your consciousness. *Nirvitarka samadhi,* as explained in 1.43, goes deeper. In this state, we focus only on the object, without any verbalization, so that the object itself becomes completely clear to us. A good example of the difference between *savitarka* and *nirvitarka* might be two different basketball players. A player who is thinking as he plays and is conscious of his own thought process may be totally focused, but he is still practicing only *savitarka samadhi.* A player who achieves such total concentration that words and thoughts fall away, and he inhabits the essence of the game with a quiet, clear consciousness, is practicing *nirvitarka samadhi.* This player is conscious without the slightest self-consciousness. He is in what many people would call "The Zone."

The second layer of *samadhi*—*vichara samadhi*—is similar to *vitarka samadhi*, but with one crucial difference: instead of something perceptible to the senses, you take as a seed object an idea or an ideal. An example might be contemplating Compassion. In *savichara samadhi*, you are absorbed in the idea of Compassion and analyze it by thinking in words. In *nirvichara samadhi*, you let the words go and become absorbed in the essence of the ideal of Compassion. This is the point at which real spiritual practice can begin. In sutra 1.47, Patanjali says that with purity of *nirvichara samadhi*, the door to Truth can open. Until that point, a person can remain in "The Zone" or contemplate great ideas and ideals but never realize that the Self exists. They can have great facility in *samadhi* and not use it for spiritual practice. Many great physicists' contemplation of important principles has taken them to *nirvichara samadhi*. Only some of them have continued that movement into contemplating the Self.

If you pass through the door that *nirvichara samadhi* opens, you arrive at the third level of *samadhi*: *ananda*, or the bliss of the Self. The seed object in *ananda samadhi* is this bliss, which is found in the Heart. Your job in *ananda samadhi* is simply to rest in the Heart and experience its bliss.

At this point, you should be asking one question: who is the perceiver of bliss? That question takes you to the fourth level of *samadhi*: *asmita*, or pure I-awareness. In this form of absorption, you go beyond bliss, which is very different from not having bliss, and relate to the recipient of bliss, the pure *buddhi* (intellect), functioning as the flawless mirror of the Self. It is crucial to remember that the Self can never be an object of contemplation because the Self is pure Subject. Even the purified intellect is still the moon, and the Self remains the sun.

By diving into our own consciousness, we can come to understand the nature of anything we contemplate. In sutra 3.4, Patanjali describes *samyama*, the process of practicing *dharana, dhyana,* and *samadhi* on the same object. To practice *samyama* is to come to know an object completely. You choose it as a seed and use it as a tool to take you deeper toward the Self. As sutra 3.5 says, when you master the process of *samyama*, the light of true knowledge appears. As sutra 3.8 makes clear, however, the process of *samyama* is external in relation to *nirbija samadhi*.

Nirbija samadhi is samadhi without any seed—consciousness without any object. The Self rests in its own nature. Sutra 1.50 establishes that, through *samprajnata samadhi*, there is the suppression of other impressions remaining in consciousness. In 1.51 Patanjali says that one attains *nirbija samadhi* by removing or eliminating all impressions, even that of *samprajnata samadhi*. At this point, the lower self is gone and the Self is revealed as the doer. This is *kaivalya*, or liberation.

The Nature of the Mind

As we have seen, what you normally call your "self" is really just the psychic instrument. This instrument is made up of three components: *manas*, which collects data from the senses; *buddhi*, the intellect or faculty of knowing, which makes decisions about the data; and *ahamkara*, the ego, which identifies with the decisions. Imagine walking down a hallway and seeing two people laughing. *Manas* takes in the scene. Your intellect then decides that the two people are laughing at someone, and it is probably you. Your ego identifies itself as the object of their laughter. Who you "are" is now miserable.

The psychic instrument interprets the vibrations that manifest from within. By the time they reach your consciousness, those vibrations have taken the form of five possible types of *vrittis*, or modifications: right knowledge, wrong knowledge, fantasy, sleep, and memory. In sutras 1.5-11, Patanjali defines all five of these thought-forms.

Right knowledge he defines as facts comprehended through direct perception, logical inference, or reliable testimony. Direct perception means perceiving something clearly on your own. Logical inference is reaching an appropriate conclusion based on clearly perceived sense data; if you smell and see smoke, and hear approaching sirens, then you can safely conclude a fire is indeed nearby. Reliable testimony may take the form of a credible witness—the trusted mechanic who says your car needs a new fuel pump—or the established truth of scripture.

Wrong knowledge is mistaking something for what it is not. The classic example is seeing a length of rope and thinking it is a snake. This sort of misapprehension applies on all levels of life. When you make decisions about people, objects, or events without truly seeing what is happening, you confuse a snake and a rope. We often see what our lower self prefers to see rather than what is really there. When we confuse things in this way, we engage in wrong knowledge. Often, wrong knowledge is a matter of labels. When we call someone who is lazy "easygoing," or someone who is meticulous "uptight," we fall into the same trap.

Fantasy is seeing something that isn't there at all, as opposed to mistaking something for what it is not. Here, there is nothing to project onto, so what you think you perceive you have actually conjured up with words. The classic example is walking down the road at night and imagining that a thief is lurking in a tree. It is not a misunderstanding—it's pure delusion. Just as a magician conjures, the person imagines, but no one else shares the delusion. Often, though, the person in the grip of fantasy will try to convince others that something nonexistent is real and that others should buy into it. This is not to say that fantasy is always bad. It gives us the power to imagine things we have not yet experienced, which helps us remain focused on our goal.

Sleep is the absence of any content in the psychic instrument. The most obvious example of this modification is dreamless sleep, because dreaming requires content. You can also experience this *vritti* while outwardly awake. Someone sitting in a boring lecture or a waiting room, not thinking about anything and not paying attention to what is going on, is asleep.

Memory is storing and recalling the experience of an object. It operates like a filing cabinet in which impressions are kept, and from which we can extract something when we choose. Obsession is one-pointed memory, in which someone keeps recalling the same impression. Like fantasy, memory can help you move toward God or take you away from God. You can remember right knowledge and valuable experiences, but you can also remember wrong knowledge or illusions.

The *vrittis* are not inherently bad. They are just how our mental machinery works. The problem is that we don't discipline them and know one from another. You have to consider how often you have used these modifications consciously rather than unreflectively. If you don't remain conscious, you will end up believing you are using right knowledge when in fact you may be using wrong knowledge, or fantasizing, or thinking you were clear and centered at a time when you were actually sleeping.

These five kinds of modifications are either painful or non-painful—but in the context of spiritual practice, these terms have unexpected meanings. A painful thought-form is one that is experienced as pleasurable or painful. When we experience pleasure, we tend to want the pleasure to continue. Because we have mistakenly linked the experience of pleasure with a particular object, we become anxious about losing our pleasure, and that anxiety is painful. As Baba used to say, one ice cream cone is pleasurable, but ten will make you sick. The experience of pleasure isn't coming from the ice cream but from within you. Whether this kind of thought-form seems painful or pleasurable, it keeps you outwardly attached and therefore produces pain, no matter how good the thought appears to be. A non-painful thought-form is one that is experienced as neutral. If a thought-form produces neither pain nor pleasure and so does not take you off track, it is neutral and therefore non-painful.

According to Patanjali, the mind is "colored" by the vibrations of what it takes in. In sutra 1.41, he establishes that in its pure state, the mind, free from all vibrations, is completely clear, like a color-less crystal. When you contemplate something, your mind takes on some of that object's vibration—some of its color. Sutra 4.17 explains that the better you know something, the more deeply its vibrations color the mind. The more the mind stills, the more clear it becomes, and the more perfectly it can take in the color of an object.

Unfortunately, until you are truly still, your lower self will react to whatever colors the mind, deluding you about your relation-ship to the world. Even your sense of why you do things will be distorted. Patanjali explains this in sutra 4.3. An incidental cause does not create a change in nature; it merely creates an opening for an existing tendency to express itself, just as a farmer irrigates a field by moving obstacles out of the water's way. We assume that what happens to us or around us causes us to act in certain ways, when in truth those incidental causes merely provide an opportu-nity for us to manifest an inner tendency. Because we don't always respond in the same way to similar situations, we know that the situations aren't really causing our reactions. This works on even the simplest levels. A three-year-old terrified by bathwater may find herself looking forward to it as an eight-year-old. The water never changed—she changed. Sometimes an ice cream cone will look delicious and at other times it might not appeal to you at all. The ice cream hasn't changed, but your relationship to ice cream has, and that is an internal event.

As you practice, you will come to see that the *buddhi*—the intellect—works like a two-sided mirror. The Self illuminates the mind (the mechanism of knowing) from one side, and the mechanism of knowing in turn takes in objects on the other side. A more common analogy is that the sun illuminates the moon, which in turn shines light on the objects around it. The moon may seem to generate its own light, but it is only reflecting the light from the sun. As Patanjali makes clear in sutras 4.19-20, we know that the mind is not self-illuminating because we can perceive it. It is itself an object, and cannot be both a subject and an object simultaneously. Sutra 4.22 puts it this way: When your consciousness is totally still, you become aware of how you have confused the Self with your mechanism of knowing. Then, having achieved *chitta-vritti-nirodha*, you experience your true nature. There is only one true Subject, and that is not the mind but the Knower of the mind. As Patanjali establishes in sutra 4.18, the unchanging Self is the master of the changing mind and knows all its modifications. All the light of consciousness comes from the Self.

Ignorance and Misery

Now that we know how the mind works, we can begin to understand why and how we end up miserable. As we have seen, Patanjali breaks down the process by which we make ourselves suffer into a series of five steps, called the *kleshas* or miseries. In sutra 2.3, he lists them: ignorance (*avidya*), loss of subject in object (*asmita*), attraction (*raga*), aversion (*dvesha*), and clinging to the life of the lower self and fearing death (*abhinivesha*). These five steps lead to all the suffering we experience. The move from *avidya* to *abhinivesha* can take place in a heartbeat. And what's worse, we choose to go down that road. But we can also choose to retrace our steps. First, we have to understand how each step works and how each leads to the next.

Avidya (ignorance) is taking the transitory to be eternal, the impure to be pure, misery to be happiness, and the non-Self to be the Self. It is the most important *klesha*, because it gives rise to all the miseries that come after it. It is the fundamental wrong knowledge. From the outset, we take an object—any object—to be permanent, when all objects are temporary. The problem is that we are unaware of our own ignorance. As a result, we move almost instantly to the second *klesha, asmita.*

The *klesha* called *asmita* (loss of subject in object) is the reverse of the *asmita* we experience in *samadhi.* It is absorption outward, away from the Self. Patanjali defines *asmita* as the false belief that our power to perceive, know, and remember is who we are. This error plunges us into what can be called a fallen existence. The intellect, which reflects the Self, decides that it is the Self, and the ego begins relentlessly affirming this decision. In our delusion, we confuse knowing with being. Once we have taken this critical step, we debase our sense of self on grosser and grosser levels. We become identified with our bodies, our relationships, our jobs, even our material possessions, and begin basing our decisions on the false identity we have constructed out of ignorance.

Once we have wrongly identified ourselves, we fall prey to *raga* (attraction) and *dvesha* (aversion). The lower self forms preferences based on its identifications. We begin to crave some things and run away from others, and we suffer as a result.

Our delusion becomes so deep that we cling for dear life to the continued existence of the lower self. This clinging, known as *abhinivesha,* is the final flowering of ignorance. In truth, the Self enlivens the lower self, but we do not even consider the possibility that the lower self is not the center of our existence. We are so sure that the lower self is the Self that we are completely unwilling to give it up. We will defend it at all costs because we believe that, if we let go of what we are attached to, we will die. We fear death, but the death of what? The Self never dies. In Truth, we can only fully live after the lower self, that collection of thought-forms, has ceased to exist.

Though we progress down the chain of the *kleshas*, we don't switch from one to the next. We add them as we go. All of them are in play at every moment. In sutra 2.4, Patanjali describes the different states in which *kleshas* operate: dominant, attenuated, alternating, and dormant. When a *klesha* is dominant, we have a good chance to see it, because, at that point, we are usually hitting a wall, providing us an opportunity for reflection. Of course, our *klesha* will have been all too apparent to those around us for some time. When a *klesha* is attenuated, it is weaker and less insistent and we are able to restrain it. Much of the time we experience *kleshas* in their alternating state, when we toggle between a *klesha's* active and latent states. If you go back and forth between craving something and losing interest in it, you are experiencing alternation. A dormant *klesha* is one that normally remains inactive but will surface in the ideal set of circumstances. Elsewhere, Patanjali discusses how, with practice, a *klesha* can be completely scorched and rendered lifeless, never to trouble us again.

The *kleshas* are the roots of our karma. What we experience in this life and in the future is based on the attachments we form because of the *kleshas* and the actions that proceed from those attachments. Sutras 2.12-14 lay out how the *kleshas* shape our lives. Karma, the cumulative effects of past actions, gives rise to experiences that are meant to teach us lessons. As long as we still have lessons to learn, we will keep having experiences. If we look at them appropriately, we can learn from them. If we don't see them clearly, we continue causing trouble for ourselves and others. We continue serving as teachers for others without ever being students ourselves. No matter how long an action, vibration, or impression has been sitting in our karmic reservoir, we will have to live it out. It will decide important things in our lives that are designed to help us grow. If we refuse to learn, we will just have the same experience again and again until we wake up.

Once we have awakened, we will see that the *kleshas* have

brought us to a life in which everything causes misery. In sutra 2.15, Patanjali explains this: The wise person, who has discrimination, sees everything as painful because everything in the world is temporary and therefore always changing and producing anxiety. We also suffer from the conflict between our temperaments and our desires, he further explains. We are discontented. We want change. We are afraid of change. We feel anxiety but don't look to the right cause. Our temperaments are, like everything else in the manifested universe, made up of the *gunas*: *tamas* (inertia, darkness, dullness, ignorance), *rajas* (activity, passion, pain, agitation), and *sattva* (brightness, clarity, calm, joy). The *gunas* combine in infinite ways, forming a spectrum of possibilities. If you are being rajasic with a strong element of *tamas*, your activity will be colored by ignorance. If you're being sattvic, your activity will be harmonious. To be truly happy, we must rise above all three *gunas*, but to do that we must first master *tamas* and *rajas* and reside in *sattva*. As with the *vrittis*, the point is to know and use the *gunas* consciously. When we are unaware, they run us, instead of the other way around. If you tend to have a rajasic temperament but must work in a library, you're going to be miserable.

But Patanjali offers good news in sutra 2.16: The pain which has not yet arrived can and should be avoided. We can choose to be free of it. To achieve that freedom, we need to know where our bondage starts. The problem, defined in sutra 2.17, is the seeming union of the Seer (the Self) with the seen (all that can be perceived)—the Subject with the object. From the moment we are born, we have forgotten our true nature, and that ignorance leads to *asmita*—we lose Subject in object. As sutra 2.18 makes clear, the whole purpose of the seen is for experience and liberation. The seen, which Patanjali also calls *prakriti*, is made up of the *gunas* and takes the form of the elements and the sense organs. The Seer, which he also calls the *Purusha*, is pure Consciousness, but in our ignorance, we think it can only see through the mind, which is really just part of *prakriti*. In this opposition of *Purusha* and *prakriti*, Patanjali's system is dualistic.

Why does any of this happen at all? Patanjali answers this in sutra 2.23: the *Purusha* appears to merge with *prakriti* as a way to become aware of itself and learn what its powers are. By coming into contact with *prakriti*, the *Purusha* also learns what powers reside in *prakriti*. The manifested universe allows the *Purusha* to play at being ignorant, discover that all *prakriti* is impermanent, and remember its own nature. The Self plays hide-and-seek with itself. Patanjali writes in sutra 2.24 that the seeming union of *Purusha* with *prakriti* happens because of ignorance. He then shows the way out of ignorance.

The Solution

Sutra 2.25 states that we are liberated when we let go of ignorance and know that we are the Seer, at which point we no longer need, or have a relationship with, the seen. We overcome our ignorance by the means prescribed in sutra 2.26: continually practice our awareness of the difference between the Self and all that is not the Self. As we now know, that practice cuts deep. All that we have ever felt or thought ourselves to be is not the Self, and therefore not Real. And, as sutra 2.28 explains, we can only realize the Self through practicing the constant awareness of the Real. Liberation does not mean that we are cut off from the manifested universe, but that we are one with it, because everything is revealed to have always been, in truth, the Seer. Liberation goes beyond all duality.

Patanjali offers two paths to liberation, one fast and one slow. The first path, known as *Ishvara-pranidhana*, is the steep way. It requires a pure and total surrender to God. Many people can do it for a moment, but precious few can sustain it. The second path is a gradual stilling of all vibrations, which unfolds over a long period of time. It is *raja yoga*.

As we saw in our discussion of the eight limbs, the practice of *raja yoga* begins with character development. In sutra 2.1, Patanjali explains that the first steps in yoga are *tapasya* (austerity), *svadhyaya* (self-study), and *pranidhanani* (working toward surrender to God). We must practice all three disciplines. When we hear the word austerity, we usually think of being deprived. The truth is that austerity removes things that distract us from the real source of happiness.

Tapasya means disciplining the senses. In *tapasya* we cook our impurities out of us as dross is removed from gold. What is left is pure. Self-study has two parts: looking at where we are, as opposed to where we believe we are, which brings us back towards the Truth; and study of scripture, which provides a context for our practice. In this sense, surrender to God means focusing on devotion, prayer, *mantra*, and remembrance of God. Complete surrender to God—letting go of the lower self—comes later, when we have achieved real non-attachment.

In sutra 2.1, Patanjali lays out the preliminary practices. We have to discipline ourselves on physical, intellectual, moral, and emotional levels. At the same time, we must study the nature of the Self and the nature of what we confuse with the Self. We need to continuously strive to surrender our will to God. These practices are all about purification, and they are designed to begin attenuating the *kleshas* and moving us toward the Self. We begin to see and then restrain the miseries of life. When we can attenuate and therefore control and stop vibrations, we can then meditate on the Self rather than on objects that take us to misery.

The process of yoga goes from restraining the modifications to controlling them and then to stilling them. As sutra 1.12 makes clear, the stilling of modifications results from persistent practice and unceasing non-attachment. When we think that some of our thought-forms are good, we believe they should not be suppressed. This indicates that we have an attachment to these forms and do not want to practice letting go of all thought-forms and achieving non-attachment. Non-attachment means just that; our lower self has no right to pick and choose attachments. That would be thought-forms deciding about thought-forms.

Practice (*abhyasa*) requires effort. But we can think that we are doing something good because we are working hard, when in fact we may be engaged in the wrong effort. Patanjali describes right effort in sutra 1.13: it is whatever exertion establishes us in the state of *chitta-vritti-nirodha*, or complete stillness. This effort will first restrain, then control, and finally still the modifications of *chitta*.

If practice is any effort that brings you to stillness, an essential piece of it is *vairagya* (non-attachment). Sutra 1.15 establishes that *vairagya* is mastery over one's own desires for what is seen and unseen. We no longer thirst after anything outside the Self. There is a saying that at the beginning of the path, we need *vairagya* and *viveka* (discernment), and at the end of the path, we need *vairagya* and *viveka*. These are not goals we strive toward, but actual disciplines we must practice at every moment. If we stand around waiting for non-attachment and discernment to come to us, we will be wasting our time.

Now, if we look at the eight limbs of classical yoga, we can see that the first five limbs are external practices, meant to lead us to the three internal practices of *dharana, dhyana*, and *samadhi*. Through the *yamas* and *niyamas*, we still our moral and emotional components and strengthen our character for the effort and focus we will need to go further. *Asana* and *pranayama* are used to still the physical body. *Pratyahara* stills the senses, readying us to be mentally one-pointed and directed inward. The inner work that follows—*dharana, dhyana*, and *samadhi*—is what we actually call the practice. This practice leads us to *nirodha*, or stillness.

If we are willing to put in the right effort to achieve *nirodha*, we need to know what obstacles we will face along the way. Patanjali supplies that information, too. Sutra 1.30 provides a list: sickness, dullness, doubt, carelessness, laziness, cravings, delusion, failure to reach a yogic stage, and inability to sustain a yogic state. These nine, and anything else that causes agitation, are obstacles to yoga. They also lead to frustration, which is a vibration on top of a vibration—in effect, agitation over a failure to still consciousness.

It is crucial to understand that these obstacles actually cause distractedness of mind, which in turn produces the symptoms Patanjali catalogs in 1.31: mental pain, depression, anxiety, restlessness, nervousness, and hard breathing. If we are experiencing these symptoms, then we have already allowed obstacles to get in the way of our practice. The symptoms don't cause the distractedness, they express it.

To prevent or remove the obstacles to yoga, we should practice what Patanjali recommends in sutra 1.32: constant awareness of one abiding truth or principle. When we focus in this way, we quiet the chatter and vibrations. The practice consists in constantly redirecting our attention inward and back to the Self.

As we redirect our attention inward, we must also transform how we relate to everything around us. In sutra 1.33, Patanjali asserts that we can clarify our minds by cultivating attitudes of friendliness toward happiness, compassion toward suffering, goodwill toward virtue, and dispassion toward vice. When we are friendly toward someone else's happiness, we can share in it. If we look on it with envy, we are cold and separate, experiencing only injury. The same is true for virtue. If we are dismissive of others' virtue, we cannot participate in it, and we are left bitter and empty. Compassion toward misery needs to arise from non-attachment, not from attachment to an ideal. True compassion does not always appear gentle. It is vitally important to be able to discriminate between misery and vice. They may look similar, but they are poles apart. Feeling compassion for vice can cause great injury to everyone concerned; it enables and perpetuates a nightmare. Anything but dispassion toward vice keeps us in relationship with it. But dispassion is not apathy: dispassion grants us detachment, while apathy not only robs us of empathy but makes us complicit in vice through our idleness.

After we have removed the obstacles to our practice, the path inward is clear, and we can do the work of returning home to the place of stillness in our true nature. The practice itself never alters. What changes is the field in which it unfolds. Eventually, we reach the place described in sutra 4.22: Once the Knower resumes the knowledge of its own nature, its consciousness does not move from place to place. We trace our way back from the perceived to the Perceiver, finally arriving where there is only the Perceiver. The faculty of knowing realizes that it is not the true Knower and never was. Sutra 4.24 describes this relationship: Though the mind is variegated by countless impressions, it is actually the agent of another, the Self, and acts in association. It experiences, senses, and thinks for the enjoyment of the Self, and the closer we get to our true nature, the more purely the mind reflects the Self. The mind's relationship to the Self is that of a soldier to a general. The general never enters the fray, but directs the soldiers from above.

Once we see the distinction between who we are and who we thought we were, between the *Purusha* and the *buddhi* (the faculty of knowing), we no longer wish to reside in something we are not. We have awakened. As sutra 4.25 says, once we realize our own true nature, as distinct from our vehicles, we stop perpetuating the false sense of self defined by our *vrittis*. We no longer want this false identity and move toward our true state of being: *kaivalya*, or abiding as the Self. Even as we make great progress, there will be lapses. Sutra 4.27 establishes that during those lapses, thoughts directed outward will arise, caused by *samskaras* (latent impressions formed by karma). *Samskaras* are subtle imprints on our vehicles made by past actions or experiences. They remain latent until an occasion arises for their expression. Even when we are far along in our practice, we must never forget *vairagya* (non-attachment) and *viveka* (discernment), because no matter how close we are to *kaivalya* (liberation), we can still lose our way. Just as we have to attenuate and render dormant the *kleshas* (afflictions), we must still all our *samskaras*.

The final step in spiritual practice is *dharma-megha-samadhi*. It is the point of no return, the place of total and permanent absorption in the Self. As sutra 4.29 establishes, to reach *dharma-megha-samadhi*, we must achieve such constant and pure non-attachment that we do not even yearn for the highest spiritual state. We have let go of all attachments. At this point, according to sutra 4.30, all *kleshas* and karmas are burned away. We are free of them. Our whole being is a transparency through which the Self, God, passes without any obstruction. We have reached liberation, which is defined in Patanjali's final sutra as the state of the Self in Itself. Total freedom and stillness. Pure Consciousness. Manifestation has fulfilled its purpose.

Chapter Sixteen

Stories of Baba, 1981-1982

Back in Ganeshpuri in 1981, my job was documentation, and I was the librarian for Baba's personal library. It was a cushy job. The fully supplied library was a huge room overlooking the courtyard. Many ashramites tried to reserve time in there, saying that they needed to do research or study. Baba closed the library—so I became the head of a library that was shut down. It was a classic example of how Baba gave people jobs because they could learn from them, not because he needed tasks performed.

I spent four hours a day in the library. It was a wonderful space, with windows all around and another floor overhead, so it stayed cool and quiet. I would lock the door from the inside, clean and dust, and read. Mostly, though, I sat on the checkout desk by the window and looked down into the courtyard at Baba. I could do that for hours. No one bothered me, and I was free from all the ashram intrigues.

I held that job for a year and a half. In the summer of 1982, during the monsoon, some of the higher-ups in the ashram asked me if I would be willing to move the library.

"It's not my library," I said. "If Baba wants to move the library, that's fine with me. It's Baba's library. I'll do whatever he wants."

The next day I heard that Baba was angry with me because he had heard that I had said it was okay to move the library. I knew the play, and knew exactly what to do. I went down to the courtyard and walked up to Baba. One of the people involved in the attempt to move the library was standing next to him, so I asked the man to translate. I named the people who had approached me, including this man, and said they had wanted me to say whether I was okay with moving the library. I repeated what I had actually said.

The man never translated.

Baba looked at me. He understood. I *pranamed* and left.

———— • ● • ————

In September of 1982, Baba held an intensive at the Taj Mahal Hotel in Bombay. Many of us came from the ashram for the program. I was seven months pregnant at the time. In Indian tradition, the baby's soul is embodied at the seventh month, so we did a *puja* for the arriving soul, and gave Baba a turban and flowers and silk and so forth.

After that intensive, Baba was very tired, but because of his love for Kashmir Shaivism, he wanted to go to Kashmir. I heard that someone had suggested that he postpone the trip, but he replied, "If I don't go now, I never will." On October 1, a few days after Baba had returned to Ganeshpuri from Kashmir, I went to speak with him about training someone to replace me as librarian when I left the job to have my baby. The next afternoon, I went for Baba's *darshan.* I knelt down in front of him. I looked up at him, and he looked back at me with absolute, unconditional love. He loved me, and I loved him. When I started to get up, he leaned over to help me.

That was the last time I saw Baba alive.

That night, at 11:02, he sat up in bed, rang for his valet, and left his body. It was the full moon.

I woke up and heard a droning over the loudspeaker. It was

"*Om Namo Bhagavate Muktanandaya*," repeated as a slow dirge.
I went to the terrace to find out what had happened, and ran into
another ashramite.

"What happened?" I asked.

"The worst."

I immediately went to the courtyard. Suddenly I was overcome with an unstoppable urge to see Baba one last time. I felt
driven, just as I did later, when I went into labor and had the urge
to push. I simply had to see Baba. Somewhere around two in the
morning, they opened his house. I was one of the first to go in.
Baba's body was sitting, not lying down. Even with my huge belly,
I did a full *pranam*, extending myself on the ground before Baba.
When I looked at him, I felt bathed in strong *shakti*. It engulfed
me. I walked out, and started to collapse. An Indian devotee I had
known for years caught me, and said, "You cannot mourn. You have
to think of the baby." Everyone was terrified that I was going to go
into labor, and they didn't want my grief to upset the baby. All the
Indian devotees—female and male—gathered around me and sup-
ported me.

The following day, people started pouring into the ashram from
around the world. Over the next few days, hundreds of thousands
came to pay their respects and view Baba's body. I didn't go to see
him again. Instead, I spent most of my time in the library. I spoke
often with Amma, who had been planning to leave the ashram the
day before Baba died but had decided to stay, and was thankful she
had. Baba's translator gave me Baba's chapati bowl, which he had
used at every meal.

Finally, the day of the funeral arrived. Baba's body was strapped
into a chair on a flatbed truck and driven into Ganeshpuri, so his
body would have a last *darshan* with Nityananda, his Guru. Then
they brought his body back and buried it. I stayed in the library
during the funeral. It was safe there, while outside people were

climbing the walls and rooting around for relics.

Baba had always said I would have a son, and that he would be born in India and have an Indian passport. I waited until my son was born and healthy enough to travel before returning to America.

For a while, I was angry with Baba for leaving me half-baked. I had experienced such bliss around him, and now I felt everything was gone. Then I started to look at what he had taught me. It hit me that I had the capacity to experience the bliss of the Self. The only time I had felt it was when I was practicing what I had learned from him. So I started doing just that.

Baba has been with me ever since.

Chapter Seventeen
Conclusion

When I first started on the path, I had many ideas, all of which turned out to be false. Reading this book may have given you lots of ideas, but if you walk away satisfied with only ideas, you will not get far along the path. Spiritual practice is not thinking the "right" thoughts, nor is it philosophy or theology. It is walking home to God. The knowledge it requires is direct perception, not thoughts. If we want to return home we must actually walk the path that so many before us have walked.

Practicing often means having your expectations shot down. You have to start from where you are on the path and move patiently toward the third level of practice. You give up your attachments to sensation and ritual when you leave the first level, let go of the mind and its ideas on moving past the second level, and dwell in the Heart at the third level, knowing that you must eventually give up even that. At every step, progress hinges on knowing where you are on the path and where you are not, who you are and who you are not.

Knowing who we are means comprehending that we are not the intellect but that which enlivens it. We must let go of "knowing" in order to know All. In letting go of all that is not the Self, we recognize that all is the Self. When we rest in the Self as the Self, we no longer perceive anything; we are everything. The illusion of separateness, from which our lower selves created their suffering, dissolves.

Be with your experience consciously, let whatever comes up within you come up, and function appropriately on the physical plane. Ground your awareness in the Heart. Be still.

Glossary

A

Abhinivesha: the last of the five afflictions (kleshas), clinging to the life of the lower self

Adivasi: a tribal person in India

Ahamkara: the ego; that part of the psychic instrument that identifies

Ananda: bliss

Ananda Samadhi: absorption with bliss as its seed

Asamprajnata Samadhi: absorption between levels of samprajnata samadhi

Asana: a yogic posture; more properly, the inner posture of resting in the Heart

Asmita: losing Subject in object; egoity

Asmita Samadhi: absorption based on the pure "I" sense

Avidya: ignorance

B

Baba: father; what we called Muktananda

Buddhi: the part of the psychic instrument that serves as the faculty of knowing

C

Chakras: energy centers or doorways in the subtle body

Chitta: the medium of Consciousness

Chitta-Vritti Nirodha: the goal of yoga; stilling the modifications of the medium of consciousness

D

Darshan: meeting

Dharana: concentration; one-pointedness

Dharma-megha-samadhi: the final state of samadhi at which liberation occurs

Dhyana: meditation

Dichotomizing: seeing things solely in terms of pairs of opposites

Dvesha: the fourth of the five afflictions (kleshas), repulsion

E

Eight Limbs of Raja Yoga: yamas, niyamas, asana, pranayama, pratyahara, dharana, dhyana, samadhi

G

Ganeshpuri: the location in India where Nityananda and then Muktananda resided

Gunas: the three constituent elements of the manifested universe (tamas, rajas, sattva)

Gurkha: a Nepalese soldier or guard; Gurkhas are legendary for their bravery

Guru: the grace-bestowing power of God; also one who conveys divine grace

H

Hatha Yoga: physical exercises or postures done for purification of the body

Heart: the ground of one's being; the point at which the unmanifest becomes manifest

I

Ishvara Pranidhana: surrender to God

J

Jesus Prayer: a Christian mantra repeated inwardly, usually taking some form of the sentence, "Lord Jesus Christ, Son of God, have mercy on me."

K

Kaivalya: the highest state reached in Patanjali's *Yoga Sutras*; liberation; aloneness

Kashmir Shaivism: a non-dualistic mystical philosophy originating in Kashmir

Karma Yoga: the path of selfless service

Kleshas: the five afflictions (ignorance, egoity, attraction, repulsion, clinging)

Kriya: a spontaneous, purifying movement of shakti in one's vehicles

Kundalini: the spiritual energy that, until awakened, lies dormant at the base of the spine

M

Mala: a string of beads to help keep track of mantras, used like a rosary

Manas: the part of the psychic instrument that collects data

Mantra: a sacred word or phrase that helps us toward liberation if we use it properly

Matrika Shakti: the power inherent in letters, which form thought-constructs that imprison us or free us, depending on our relation to them

Muktananda: a great modern saint; Rohini's teacher

N

Nirbija Samadhi: absorption without a seed

Nirvichara Samadhi: absorption in the essence of an abstract seed object, without thought constructs

Nirodha: bringing to stillness

Nirvitarka Samadhi: absorption in the essence of a material seed object, without thought-constructs

Niyamas: the second limb of Raja Yoga; observances

O

Orthodox Christian: the Christian tradition dominated by Greek and Slavic churches

P

Patanjali: the great Indian saint who wrote down the *Yoga Sutras*; lived c.150 BCE

Prakriti: nature; the manifested world

Pranam: prostration as a gesture of reverence

Pranayama: control of one's vital energy, which rides the breath

Pratyahara: the fifth limb of Raja Yoga; conscious withdrawal of the five senses

Psychic Instrument: the mind, made up of manas, buddhi, and ahamkara

Puja: worship; ritual

Purusha: in Raja Yoga, the Witness, the Self

R

Raga: the third of the five kleshas; attraction

Raja Yoga: the yoga of eight limbs (see Eight Limbs)

Rajas: the guna of activity

S

Sabija Samadhi: absorption with attributes

Sadhana: spiritual practice; the means for attaining liberation

Sahaj Samadhi: walking bliss; continuous absorption in God

Samadhi: the process of absorption in Yoga

Samprajnata Samadhi: absorption with a seed object

Samskara: a latent impression; karmic residue

Samyama: the process of concentration, meditation, and absorption practiced together

Sat-Chit-Ananda: Absolute Truth, Absolute Consciousness, and Absolute Bliss; God's nature

Sattva: the guna of brightness and calm

Savichara Samadhi: absorption with an abstract seed object

Savitarka Samadhi: absorption with a material seed object

Self: our true nature; pure Subject

Seva: action performed as service

Shakti: cosmic power; spiritual energy

Shaktipat: the awakening of the kundalini; the descent of divine grace

Shiva Sutras: a central text of Kashmir Shaivism, written down by Vasugupta around the 10th century CE

St. Simeon the New Theologian: an Orthodox saint who lived in

the 10th century CE and wrote parts of the *Philokalia*
Sufi: a mystic of the Muslim tradition, though Sufism may in fact predate Islam
Sutra: aphorism; thread
Svadhyaya: self-study; study of sacred scriptures

T

Tai Chi Chuan: "the ultimate fist"; an internal martial art based on inner energy (chi)
Tamas: the guna of inertia, darkness, and ignorance
Tapasya: austerities; practices designed to purify
Torah: the five books of Moses, sacred in the traditions of Judaism

V

Vairagya: non-attachment
Vichara Samadhi: absorption based on analysis, with an abstract seed object
Vitarka Samadhi: absorption based on sense experience, with a material seed object
Viveka: discernment; discrimination
Vrittis: modifications; vibrations of chitta

W

Wu-wei: "non-doing"; in Taoism, acting from the Self rather than from the lower self; total surrender to and immersion in the Tao

Y

Yamas: the first limb of Raja Yoga; abstentions
Yoga: "union"; the process that leads to oneness with the Self

Aphorisms

We become what we meditate on. Meditate on God.

When people lose control of their minds, they seek to gain power over others.

Low and high self-esteem are both egotistical.

Nice is often a euphemism for victim.

Putting up with something is not forgiveness.

Discipline from the ego is behavior modification. Discipline from the Heart is personal transformation.

Numbing is not being cool or in control. It doesn't even fool the world, does it?

Worrying is a form of numbing.

Abandonment is conflict without the other person.

The nurtured soul brings fulfillment; the nurtured ego, abuse.

People in pain win the dependency game.

If I weren't worthless, I'd be a nothing.

Lying is not conflict resolution.

"I thought it, so you must have heard it."

"Positive feelings" are those that do not challenge or threaten your limited sense of self.

Ego and pretense are mistaken for intelligence.

Will others like you more if you like you less?

Do you feel like a winner only when there is a loser?

Relating from the mind is win/lose; relating from the Heart is win/win.

To give up failure, you have to give up success.

In the power plays within a pair, the one who initiates contact is inferior.

If need equals love, then love thrives on incompetence.

The goal is to continue to love the process.

When you're in your mind, you can't use your intellect.

Being cut off from our feelings makes us behave irrationally.

"Your life doesn't exist when I'm not there."

You take your problems with you, so why go anywhere?

The spark of ego gets mistaken for the spark of freedom.

Silence is not always peace, and peace is not always silent.

Compassion is love with detachment.

Dispassion is detachment with compassion.

Don't fix people. Encourage people to fix themselves.

We are responsible for speaking out, not for whether others hear what we say.

Repentance is not guilt. It is awakening.

Everything in you is in the others; everything in the others is in you.

There is nowhere where spiritual growth is not possible.

Clean up the outside by first cleaning up the inside.

Sentiments are of the mind; true feelings are of the Heart.

Do you love others, or just your concept of others?

Simple is not dumb.

Rebel against your wrong understanding, not against Reality.

It defies reason that an unreasonable proposition, reasonably expressed, is received as reasonable.

A reasonable proposition, unreasonably expressed, is still reasonable, though unreceived.

Trusting words alone and not the experience behind them brings disaster.

Only when the mind loses control of you can you gain control of it.

The degree to which life works is the degree to which we are honest.

Discrimination and discernment are judgment purified.

To love with respect is to love without attachment.

I am, therefore I can think.

The real world is wherever you are Real.

Surrendering to God is a sign of strength, not weakness.

Surrendering to God does not rob us of personality or vitality.

To rest within the Heart and look out at the world is to see as God sees.

One hundred percent (fe)male is only fifty percent human.

Discipline is the vessel from which all creativity pours.

Insights and breakthroughs are like seedlings: untended, they bear no fruit.

Romance is the invitation to relationship, not the goal.

Romance is how grown-ups play make-believe.

The path to God is long, arduous, and joyful; the path to personal power is short, facile, and deadly.

Shoveling the dirt out of the mind lightens the load of the Heart.

The mind has a mind of its own that has a mind of its own that has a mind of its own.

A calm ocean lies beyond the storm of boredom.

Go into the darkness and the darkness is dissolved.

Bring into harmony how you feel about yourself, how you think you come across, and how others perceive you.

Keep the mind quiet so you can hear what God says.

Deep secrets make our alienation special.

Divestment of attention is not divestment of responsibility.

No matter how many times you've been born, someday you have to grow up.

Guilt is the acceptable alternative to unacceptable feelings.

Destiny can't change, but your attitude can.

Enthusiasm is a fair-weather friend.

Deception is nobody's friend. Has it ever worked for you?

Narcissism is when people look outside themselves into their minds for happiness.

A pleaser avoids conflict, only to end up creating it. What you run from, you run into.

There's a difference between standing up for yourself and indulging your desires.

You are who and what you complain about.

Your value is not in what you do but in who you are.

It's the job of inferior people to keep superior people in their place.

The way to be superior is to be equal.

The way to always be right is to admit when you're wrong.

If we are in harmony with the ego, we are out of sync with Reality.

Look within. It's the only way out.

Suggested Readings

The Aphorisms of Siva. Trans. Mark S. G. Dyczkowski. Ed. Paul E. Muller-Ortega. New Delhi: Indica Books, 1998.

The Art of Prayer. Trans. E. Kadloubovsky and E. M. Palmer. Ed. Timothy Ware. London: Faber and Faber, 1997.

The Bhagavadgita. Trans. S. Radhakrishnan. New Delhi: Harper Collins, 1998.

Boehme, Jacob. *The Way to Christ.* Trans. Peter Erb. New York: Paulist Press, 1978.

Chryssavgis, John. *In the Heart of the Desert.* Bloomington, IN: World Wisdom, 2003.

Eckhart, Meister. *Meister Eckhart: The Essential Sermons, Commentaries, Treatises, and Defense.* Ed. Edmund Colledge, Bernard McGinn, Houston Smith. New York: Paulist Press, 1981.

Eliot, T. S. *Four Quartets.* New York: Harvest Books, 1968.

Lao-Tzu. *Taoteching.* Trans. Red Pine. San Francisco: Mercury House, 1996.

Maneri, Sharafuddin. *The Hundred Letters.* Trans. Paul Jackson S.J. New York: Paulist Press, 1980.

McGuckin, John Anthony, ed. *The Book of Mystical Chapters.* Trans. John Anthony McGuckin. Boston: Shambhala, 2002.

Merton, Thomas, and Zi Zhuang, ed. *The Way of Chuang Tzu.* Trans. Thomas Merton and Zi Zhuang. New York: New Directions, 1965.

Merton, Thomas, ed. *The Wisdom of the Desert.* Trans. Thomas Merton. New York: New Directions, 1960.

The Principal Upanisads. Trans. S. Rhadakrishnan. New York: Humanities Press Inc., 1978.

Radhakrishnan, S., and Charles A. Moore, eds. *A Sourcebook in Indian Philosophy*. Princeton, N.J.: Princeton University Press, 1989.

Richard of St. Victor. *Richard of St. Victor: The Twelve Patriarchs, the Mystical Ark, Book Three of the Trinity*. Trans. Grover A. Zinn. New York: Paulist Press, 1979.

Siva Sutras: The Yoga of Supreme Identity. Trans. Jaideva Singh. Delhi, India: Motilal Banarsidass Publishers, 1995.

Swami Hariharananda Aranya. *Yoga Philosophy of Patanjali*. Albany: State University of New York Press, 1983.

Swami Lakshmanjoo. *Shiva Sutras: The Supreme Awakening*. Ed. John Hughes. Culver City, CA: Universal Shaiva Fellowship, 2002.

Swami Muktananda. *I Am That*. South Fallsburg, NY: SYDA Foundation, 1992.

---. *Kundalini: The Secret of Life*. 2nd ed. South Fallsburg, NY: SYDA Foundation, 1994.

---. *Mystery of the Mind*. South Fallsburg, NY: SYDA Foundation, 1981.

---. *Play of Consciousness*. San Francisco: Harper & Row, 1978.

---. *Secret of the Siddhas*. Trans. Swami Chidvilasananda. South Fallsburg, NY: SYDA Foundation, 1994.

---. *Siddha Meditation*. Oakland, CA: SYDA Foundation, 1975.

---. *Where are You Going?* South Fallsburg, NY: SYDA Foundation, 1981.

Swami Prabhavananda, and Christopher Isherwood. *How to Know God: The Yoga Aphorisms of Patanjali*. Hollywood, CA: Vedanta Press, 1981.

Swami Vishnu Tirtha Maharaj. *Devatma Shakti*. 5th ed. Delhi,

India: Yoga Peeth Trust, 1980.

Taimni, I. K. *The Science of Yoga.* Adyar, India: The Theosophical Publishing House, 1961.

Teresa of Ávila. *Interior Castle.* Trans. E. Allison Peers. Ed. E. Allison Peers. New York: Image Books, 2004.

Underhill, Evelyn. *Mysticism.* Oxford: Oneworld, 1999.

The Upanishads. Trans. Swami Nikhilananda. III ed. Vol. I–IV. New York: Ramakrishna-Vivekananda Center, 1990.

Vijnanabhairava, or Divine Consciousness. Trans. Jaideva Singh. Delhi, India: Motilal Banarsidass, 1991.

The Way of a Pilgrim. Trans. R. M. French. San Francisco: HarperSanFrancisco, 1965.

Whicher, Ian. *The Integrity of the Yoga Darsana.* Albany: State University of New York Press, 1998.

Writings from the Philokalia *on Prayer of the Heart.* Trans. E. Kadloubovsky and G. E. H. Palmer. New York: Faber and Faber, 1995.

Acknowledgements

This book has had many helpers along the way. Though I respectfully refrain from using most of their names in the text, my Guru brothers and sisters have been essential to my *sadhana*; we all played parts for each other in the great teaching drama orchestrated by our Baba.

My current students, especially the members of my weekly Lessons and Questions class, offered valuable feedback on evolving drafts of the book. Clara Marin, John Pollara, and Jim Condron put in extraordinary effort and skill, going through the manuscript with care and conviction.

My sons, Ian and Aaron Ralby, having grown up with my teaching and these stories, provided moral support, unstinting encouragement, and expert feedback.

Finally, I want to thank my husband, David Soud, who typed, shared, and wrestled with me to help bring forth my authentic voice—a voice that would express some portion of what Baba has given me and continues to give me.

About the Author

Rohini Ralby began walking home early, not quite sure where or which way to go. Until she could find the right teacher, she had to rely on her own effort. By the time she was 21, her main focus was dance. Her teachers at Washington University in St. Louis, especially Annelise Mertz and Leslie Laskey, stripped her of her superficial notions about dance, art, and architecture. Graduate school took her to the San Francisco Bay area for an advanced degree in dance. The search for her movement, her authentic expression, led her to Tai Chi, which she studied intensively in Berkeley with T. R. Chung, a student of the great master Kuo Lien Ying.

After graduate school, Rohini returned to her hometown of Boston and opened a successful Tai Chi Chuan school in Cambridge. She also studied Chinese language and earned a degree in acupuncture. While practicing Tai Chi Chuan, she had a powerful experience of floating, wholeness, and freedom; when not practicing, she felt small and incomplete. She wanted the experience she had practicing Tai Chi Chuan all the time, even when cleaning the toilet. Every year, she spent a month in California studying with Chung. On one visit, as soon as she walked in the door he told her, "You're finished here. Go to him."

"Him" was Swami Muktananda. Rohini's eight years with Muktananda, affectionately known as Baba, taught her exactly what she was looking for. She wanted to work only with him, so she made sure that she could be with him most of the time during those eight years. She was in charge of security for the ashram in Ganeshpuri, India; she stood with him in the ashram courtyard; and she was his appointments secretary for most of his second world tour. Whatever needed doing, she did. All these roles taught her how to deconstruct her old ways of operating and relate to the world appropriately.

Where Rohini mainly learned the practice was at the back stair of Baba's house in Ganeshpuri. For years, every day after lunch, her job was to stand by Baba's back stair. He would come out and sit on the steps. She would stand by the stair and protect his privacy. Though from the outside it looked as if nothing was happening, he was teaching her inwardly. She learned how to be aware of the outside while constantly boring into the core of her being. Then she would rest there, as deep in as she could go at the time. Baba also spent hours in the courtyard, and Rohini's job was to stand nearby in case he needed something. There, she practiced what she had learned.

After Baba left his body in 1982, Rohini returned to America. Baba had taught her the practice; now she simply needed to do it, burn up the ignorance that was preventing her from knowing who she really is, and again experience the bliss she had felt in Baba's presence.

For many years, no matter what happened on the outside, whether giving birth to her two sons, helping them to manhood, or enduring and then leaving an unhealthy environment, Rohini just practiced, knowing that whatever God does He does for good. Through all the years, Baba has been with her, guiding her on her walk.

For the past two decades, Rohini has quietly worked as a spiritual director. Though she has written and privately published for her students a short book titled *A Spiritual Survival Kit*, *Walking Home with Baba* is her first mass-market publication. Rohini intends her next book to present a spiritual approach to parenting.